D0708082

Ian Paisley My Father

Ian Paisley My Father

Rhonda Paisley

Marshall Pickering

Marshall Morgan and Scott
Marshall Pickering
3 Beggarwood Lane, Basingstoke, Hants RG23 7LP, UK

First published in 1988 by Marshall Morgan and Scott
Publications Ltd
Part of the Marshall Pickering Holdings Group
A subsidiary of the Zondervan Corporation

British Library in Publication Data

ISBN: 0 551 01722 8

Text set in Linotron Bembo by Input Typesetting Ltd, London
Printed in Great Britain by Richard Clay, Bungay

Contents

For Mum and Dad with all my Love

Foreword

It has been said that the only important thing a writer needs is a subject. If that is true then this book by Rhonda Paisley was a book begging to be written.

Across the world Ian Paisley's name is synonomous with Unionist politics. He is adored by many, abhorred by others but cannot be ignored. He has won a place in the pages of the history of N. Ireland. Academics, former political colleagues, and political journalists have written numerous books and articles claiming to depict the real Ian Paisley, what motivates him and what kind of person he really is.

To those who know him much of what has been written has been petty, malicious, speculative and utterly untruthful. Indeed after reading much of what has been written I have often wondered whether the person described is really the Ian Paisley I know, because to those who work with him the 'Big Man' is not the fiery rabble rouser, demanding dictator or intolerant bigot described by many of the 'authorities' who have written long articles, dissertations, or books about him, rather he is a kind man, full of fun, humorous and above all straightforward and honest in his dealings.

The best picture of what a man is really like can be obtained by his family. They see him in all circumstances under all kinds of situations and when there is no need for pretence.

In this book Rhonda gives a candid picture of what her dad is really like not only as a politician and a preacher but also as a parent. Her writing shows that she has inherited many of her daddy's characteristics. It is humorous, honest and passionate.

She is completely frank about the difficulties and frustrations of being brought up in a family which is always in the public eye and the unrealistic demands which are made upon members of the family.

The book goes beyond being just an account of life as Ian Paisley's daughter. Rhonda shows how her father's influence, her own personal faith and events in our country have affected her own beliefs. I am sure that many will find her independence both surprising and refreshing.

This book is a good read and makes an important contribution towards understanding one of Ulster's most controversial characters.

Alderman Samuel Wilson B.Sc.Econ (hons)

Introduction

By profession I am an artist, not a writer, so I cannot promise that in reading this book you will find it either eloquent in style or racey in its imaginative dimension. Art expresses itself without words and it is not easy to change from one form of expression to another. My father has been the subject of much interest for as long as I have memory. I suppose that is why you have chosen to read this book and why I find myself writing it!

The artist Domenichino, when blamed for his slowness in finishing a picture replied, 'I am continually painting it within myself'. This is often how I felt while writing this book. No doubt most others in the course of writing feel exactly the same. It is not a biographical work by any means, nor was it ever intended to be so. It is a little dander through the experience of our family, and traces for you, I hope, a lively, honest and colourful pattern of the gift of life we share as a family.

My thanks are to the publishers who approached me with the proposal and in particular to Christine Whitell, the editor under whom I worked. Also to my Mum who corrected my spellings and as a result has enough material to write her own book on that subject alone! To Paul Handley for his invaluable criticism and professional advice. To my family for their encouragement and help and, of course, to 'the Big Man' himself for being my father and leading such a life of interest, dedication and achievement.

Rhonda Paisley
Belfast, 1988

CHAPTER ONE

Family

My view of Ian Paisley is always that of a daughter. My opinions of his words and actions are coloured strongly by this bond. It is a bond of which I have never been embarrassed nor ashamed. I love my father and no matter what he says or does I shall always love him. It is true that I find much in common between his beliefs and those which I have come to hold myself. It is also true that I feel as much ease in being frank with him when our views differ as when we are in agreement. That I think is a good element in a parent-child relationship and one not easy to achieve when raising children. I believe Dad would have it no other way than that his children hold beliefs which they know to be first reconciled with God and then to defend and uphold those views to others, himself included. My family background to the outsider may seem like a curious blend of politics and preaching, of ministers and activists, of protests and propaganda – and indeed I must accept that it is. Often I look around me in the middle of a protest to find I am flanked by uncles, aunts, cousins, and of course brothers and sisters! But my background has created a unique and privileged upbringing for me.

There are seven members in my immediate family including Mum and Dad (and we always have a pet dog!). As they will be mentioned frequently I shall introduce them to you now.

The eldest child is Sharon, two years my senior. She is married to John Huddleston. Sharon is to me what I suppose all older sisters are to their younger sisters – perfect! For me, Sharon's steady nature and her very sure faith have always been an inspiration. Often where I would waver, Sharon remains strong and where I would question, she would accept. These two elements in her character have been an immense example to me as I grew up alongside her, and continue to be so now into adult life when I'm afraid I still waver and question. John, her husband has a character much the same and for us as a family 'he can do no wrong'. They have one child (so far!) – a blonde, blue-eyed girl called Lydia Sharon Jane. Until her birth in May 1986, I never comprehended the precious gift of life to the extent I understand it now. The beauty of a relationship between two people which unites to give life surely is worth every effort to protect it. The same year as Lydia's birth, a friend of mine underwent two abortions. She is a young unmarried girl. The stark contrast between these two events left an indelible mark on my life. Agony versus joy, guilt versus freedom, bitterness verses gentleness, remorse versus love. I wish I could have somehow avoided that lesson.

Cherith is my younger sister – I am number two in the family. She is six years younger than me. Until I returned home after four years at university in America, Cherith was always my 'baby sister'. In many ways I missed her growing-up years though I did detect a change in her letters. The theme had shifted from asking for advice on apple orchard raids to inquiring about perfume, from playing jokes on teachers to mentioning the good-looking boys around. Being home again, and with Sharon happily married, naturally Cherith and I became very close. We have much in common like Greenpeace and 'No Nukes' and vegetarianism – mere trivia to the rest of the family! I honestly think we tell each other everything – well, almost!

To finish off the children – unless Mum and Dad change their plans radically! – are Kyle and Ian, one year and one month younger than Cherith. How to describe these two is beyond me. Kyle is ten minutes Ian's senior. He is very sensitive in nature but also immovable once he makes a decision. Kyle has the uncanny knack of saying the right thing but at the wrong time. A former baby-sitter once flaunted a photograph of her own children taken in a rather dilapidated part of their back yard. The kids, grubby, tired and hungry-looking, were being embraced by their bedraggled mother. As she took it from her album she said proudly, 'Would you look at the state of that'. Kyle looked, and to my mother's horror commented, 'Rising damp'. (He was the grand old age of five.)

Ian is just as sensitive in nature as Kyle but in a different way and over different things. He too is immovable when he believes in something. I always remember when he was younger he was having an in-depth discussion about the troubles with Mum, Sharon and me. With the clear and confident logic of a politically-aware eight-year-old he affirmed, 'What this country needs is a dictator, and I'm the man to do it!' His political awareness is no less astute but his logic, I'm glad to say, has matured somewhat. My two brothers are the best any sister could wish for. They are humorous, loving and very caring. On these merits I can turn a blind eye to their more normal male attributes, such as leaving shaving foam in the wash hand basin and their desire to be waited on hand and foot!

The five of us grew up close. We were always taught to show our love to each other and to regard ourselves as part of a family unit. The unity we had as youngsters has grown as we have grown and now as adults – all in our twenties – we enjoy the loyalty one to another which our formative childhood years taught us. The situation in Ulster and Dad's ever-increasing public profile played a strong role in this aspect of our home life. These two elements remain a constant and intricate part of our living, making things seem forever in a state of flux. Whole weeks are turned upside-down by events, holidays are altered suddenly by changing situations – in fact seldom a day goes by that is not affected by the political cut and thrust. Sometimes I envy those whose lives seem to tick on untouched, but my envy is short-lived. This has been the norm for us and anyway I cannot change it. The right attitude to your lot is the key to many things.

My mother, of course, has always been there. An obvious

statement maybe, but the greatest compliment a child can pay. Mum is brilliant. She is fun, lively – and spits fire when she is angry! But she is gently profound in her understanding of us and careful to arrange her life always with Christ first. My mother was actively involved in political life before Dad, being encouraged by him to run for Local Council. This she did in 1957 and served on the Belfast Corporation, as it then was, for seven and a half years. A small section of her old constituency falls into the area which I represent at present on Belfast Council.

Mum is as busy as Dad and always has been. After serving on the Council she was elected to the Northern Ireland Convention and later to the Northern Ireland Assembly. While no longer a public representative, she has no lighter a schedule. As the wife of a moderator and minister, she speaks frequently at religious meetings throughout Ulster. As the Party leader's wife she has many and varied functions to attend and engagements to carry out. She keeps my father's mail all channelled in the right direction (a day's work in itself) and does the same with Dad and the rest of us!

If anything makes me angry it is hearing some self-righteous, pristine, dull individual level criticism at my mother about herself, her husband or her family. To be honest I'm often tempted to make a certain gesture at such people just to relieve my feelings and enjoy the reaction! My restraint is yet another instance of my mother's good influence; knowing that she would be upset holds me back, and I am thankful that her teaching to ignore such criticism curbs my waywardness – a little!

Mum is the perfect partner for Dad. Their marriage has its foundation in Christ. He is the head of their home and so when separation comes as it has in our home, and when the way in front is not clear, as is often the case in Ulster, their rock has never collapsed into quicksand nor their hope into despair.

Mum and Dad's friendship began when Mum was only seventeen – there are six years between them in their ages. They had only been dating for three weeks when Dad proposed. That is just my Dad all over – he is excellent at decision-making and acts with confidence afterwards when turning his decision into a reality. There are many similarities in their characters and their backgrounds, both coming from strong, close-knit families.

Dad was born in the city of Armagh in 1926 and at the age of two the family moved to Ballymena where my grandfather's pastorate continued in Hill Street Baptist Church in the town.

As a young man Dad had two interests, one in farming and the other, the sea. He wanted as a career to be a sea captain. He preached his first sermon at just sixteen years of age, however, and his calling to the Gospel ministry was established in his life.

He went on to study in The Barry School of Evangelism in the Rhondda Valley in Wales (from where my name was chosen as a result) and then spent three years in the Reformed Presbyterian Theological Hall in Belfast. He has been the victim of much scorn over his qualifications. He holds an honorary Doctorate of Divinity from the Bob Jones University – which he did not buy despite the usual remark! – and he is a Fellow of the Royal Geographical Society. The other letters after his name are MP and MEP! His detractors have been a little quieter after his voting record in the elections for the European Parliament took him into the Guinness Book of Records, for the highest ever individual vote polled in the British Isles.

As well as being a European MP, he is also leader of the Democratic Unionist Party, which he formed in 1971 and which now speaks for a good half of all Unionist voters in Northern Ireland. His first love, though, has to be for the Free Presbyterian Church of Ulster which he was again instrumental in forming twenty years before, in 1951. On a typical Sunday, he leads the three services at his own Ravenhill Church and also preaches to one or two of the other fifty Free Presbyterian congregations in Ulster – and that is not mentioning the mid-week meetings.

His media image, though, has grown up largely round his political activities, in particular during elections, of which Ulster seems to make a regular habit! The press paints a fiery and flame-coloured portrait. Energy and heat come through the strongest. Passionate zeal whirls through its brushstrokes. All these are part of my father's character but they have been magnified instead of laid alongside his other, equally strong, merits. Newspaper photographs and television clips, all show him in full passionate flight. The big-hearted, outgoing enthusiasm of the man is seldom touched upon. But in reality the fire is controlled by the vision which has ignited it; the flame is tempered by the love he has for his fellow citizens. The energy is channelled, not wayward; the heat is from strength, not temper. Passion is nothing to be ashamed of when it is set not to arouse wickedness but to conquer it.

Dad is not a noisy person – though I cannot expect his critics to agree with me. Amazing as it might seem, I never think of him as loud even when I hear the loudness he is famous for. I suppose the child of a chimney sweep never thinks of her father as dirty even when he is covered in soot. It is his job and the soot comes with it. Forthright expression is part of what my father is involved in and the volume comes with it. What more can I say? – to me it is that simple. He talks too straight for many, and yet has survived in Ulster's political arena longer than any other.

In many ways the gifts of oratory and leadership which Dad has are from nature. He is 'a natural' as people say; but the perfecting of these gifts has been wrought by self-culture and a lot of work. For my father, the touchstone has been his obedience to God. The pleasure of the pursuit has kept him humble-minded and warmed his achievements with love. This leads to the ability to enjoy life and laugh as much at himself as at other things – an impossible characteristic to resist in any person.

One of the most pleasing aspects of Dad for me is his total disregard of persons when it comes to something like a joke. If they cannot take it as a laugh then they are not worth bothering about. This attitude is also reflected by Dad when it comes to major matters. If he believes something then he will set his sights and go for it no matter who he has to face on the way. I love that attitude, for it embraces totally the belief that all men are equal and no person, just because they are adorned by society's labels, has any right from preventing anyone setting out and achieving what they believe in. That is why people respect my father. He is vibrant in his attack, cunning when necessary, open-minded and open-hearted to others' needs, but never distracted from his goal nor sidetracked by what people may think. How often as a child I listened to other parents base their whole arguments against something on 'what the neighbours would think'! Thank God that Mum and Dad never were so much concerned with what anybody thought as much as they were with how we believed in our heart on the matter.

There are outrageous statements made, you know, about his wealth. He is said to own ranches in Australia and Canada. We are supposed to live off the weekly church collections (which, incidentally, are said to be lifted in buckets!). He is supposed to own every property of the Free Presbyterian Church so that 'come the revolution' we will all escape with the lolly!

In truth Dad is a generous man, generous in every sense of the word. He is not a man who is concerned about riches. His attitude is much like that of the artist Michaelangelo, who said of another painter whose motivation was to earn riches, 'I think he will be a poor fellow so long as he shows such an extreme eagerness to become rich'.

As children we had to mature early in many ways. It was the only way we could cope with the vast gap between the father we knew and the picture painted of him by others. Somehow this gap had to be comprehended and teaching us this can have been no easy task for my parents. I suppose we had to yield sooner our whimsical childhood hours than did our peers. We learnt while younger than most that life can be lonely and hard when someone close is 'public property'. Yet all this was well compensated for by the fact that our parents developed and established a privacy within our home that permitted us to be theirs with as much importance as any child could need to feel under the growing pressures of both religious and public life.

And Dad continues to be my friend and adviser. He knows me. He ascertains what I am asking, needing or cannot express.

It is this nearness in our individual relationships with him as children which has prevented us ever becoming lost to him despite the fact that he is more times physically away from us than with us. Several years ago I recall distinctly realising this side of our relationship. I was away from home at the time and had broken up with a boyfriend. Our friendship had been very close, and because I valued it so much, it was impossible for me to find expression for the feelings which resulted. When friendship develops its trust faithfully, and that trust ripens to yield rare fruits of understanding, honesty, pleasure and love, its removal brings many withdrawal symptoms!

Having not come to terms with the situation within myself, I dreaded the task of telling someone else, even Dad. Dad was coming to visit while on a preaching tour, and I knew he would ask about my boyfriend. The moment is well branded in my memory. I have often wondered whether he recalls it because we have never talked about it since. Anyway, there we were in Dad's room, unpacking his case and talking happily about everything at once, as in the tendency when you have not seen someone for a while. Casually Dad asked how my friend was. There was no huge silence, no tears, no not-knowing-where-to-look scene.

'We don't see each other any more,' I replied. Dad paused from unpacking, looked at me over the top of the case and said very tenderly, 'You've learnt in a hard school, love,' and we went on talking.

He may not have known the reasons or the circumstances, but he knew nonetheless exactly what my words meant. The comfort I needed as his child – and the relief that I had absolutely no need to explain anything in order to get that comfort – were all wrapped up in his one sentence. From that point I began to come to terms with something which had seemed insurmountable and I gained a fraternal union with Dad which continues to enrich my life. In maturing from girlhood to womanhood, I could never repay my father's understanding and my mother's example.

CHAPTER TWO

Upbringing

A child's upbringing inevitably reflects that particular generation's thought and social standards. Likewise it mirrors the personal views and prejudices of its parents. The tones of these reflections are the child's own character, and the hues which they cast ought to be developed in freedom of thought and conscience.

Dad's upbringing was much stricter than ours, and ours was much stricter than our friends'. As a matter of fact, any doubts which I have concerning my faith find their root in the question of upbringing. Were I another man's daughter what would be my views of Christ and redemption? Were my father not involved politically, would I hold some of the opinions and beliefs that I do? The only fact which alleviates this nagging doubt is that in order to win my soul, Christ placed me in the home that he did so that I could learn the way of salvation. I know other ministers' children who find this fact as sweet a comfort as I do.

That Dad was the son of a minister is of immense help to us; that Mum was not, is so as well. Ministers' children the world over find there are a host of pressures upon them and many criticisms levelled at them. Unfair? Granted, but unchanging it seems from generation to generation. The minister's offspring is pictured as pious beyond belief. He or she has a natural ability to 'walk' Sunday School exams. They are never disobedient, insubordinate or rude. They sing nothing but hymns and spend leisure hours after school praying! Of course the minister's child never attains this ideal drummed into the minds of their peers, so they are peeled, strip by strip by the same tongue that fashioned the ideal. The rancid criticism that results produces cynicism and hardness in all concerned. Thankfully, for every one such critic, there are two who encourage the minister's children. Unfortunately it is the one which leaves a stronger impression than the two. It is the sting of an insect that impresses, not its delicately fashioned wings nor its finely coloured body.

Why my father was raised with what I can only see as a narrower perspective on life, has to do with the generation he comes from, because the principles he sought to instil in us are no different. After all, the Ten Commandments have not altered! To conclude that the differences are any deeper is not realistic. Differences in our upbringing have no moral foundation. They are superficial. For example, my father would never have been allowed a snooker table, nor would he ever have been permitted to go and play the game. Snooker for us is no more of a deal than a game of snakes and ladders. I think my Grandmother Paisley must have held a similar view on horseriding. When I took up the sport at ten years of age her response upon seeing me in jodhpurs was that it would be a source of trouble. The only trouble it caused me were a few hard landings – and those, it might be argued, knocked a bit of sense into me!

Of course there are many things which in and of themselves are by no means wrong but set out of place in our lives they can become detrimental. Here we have the supposed dilemma, for what may damage one person does not necessarily affect another. Many Christians choose to ignore this individuality among believers. What is wrong for them is wrong for all, and often the partaker is condemned as 'backslidden'. Dad and I hold quite different views on the theatre. He does not attend, nor ever has attended plays and similar productions. Frankly, he does not particularly like any of us doing so either. But when we became adults he gave us freedom of choice. We have no need to hide where we go or do not go. I know many

young Christians whose parents have similar views on such
things and instead of being reasonable they secretly go where
they want and, while not directly lying about the matter, they
avoid giving a straight answer as to where they were. I find live
performance extremely enjoyable (that is, with the exception of
opera). Dad does not share this view. The mutual respect we
hold for each other's opinion is no hardship on either of us and
certainly he does not consider me unregenerate because of it!
No wonder the church everywhere has not excelled when such
legal tenants behave as though they are the only ones who
know the Landlord!

While my grandparents were strict in their views it is sweet
relief that they were not of this vein of thinking either. In fact
every leader of Fundamentalism I have met through Dad's
ministry has been opposed to this type of condemnation of
fellow believers or indeed of fellow human beings. Those who
opt for it prove that they are genius when it comes to the letter
of the law but retards when it comes to its spirit. The image
of moderation depicts weakness to them, not balance and
harmony. Blatant dictatorship of a personal view creates frustration and insecurity – perfect conditions for Satan to get to
work.

Experiencing the blend of family life which permits room
for us each as individuals brings deep appreciation for my
grandparents who, in their respective homes, raised their children with a clear and balanced view of life. And this they gave
to more than just Mum and Dad. My mother has a sister and
two brothers, while Dad has a brother and a sister. I have
fourteen first cousins. As they in turn have married, their
husbands, wives and children have joined our broadening
family circle, bringing joy and a lively new dimension.

My paternal grandfather was a patient and gentle man. He
was tall with a fine complexion and white hair. He wore glasses
and used a walking stick. He never went out without his hat
– in fact this is one thing all my grandparents had in common:
they all wore hats! I remember as a child when I tried to
imagine what God looked like I thought he looked like Papa
Paisley!

When we were young Papa suffered a stroke which left him with impaired speech. His mind was not affected by this and until he died he was very astute. Papa always had two bags of sweets in his pockets – one of Mint Imperials and the other of cinnamon lozenges. When he stayed with us during summer holidays he always came upstairs after Mum had put us into bed, to kiss us goodnight and give us one of each type of sweet. My poor mother would have to persuade us to surrender them to her until the morning for fear we would choke to death in bed!

There is only one occasion in my memory of hearing Papa speak. At the conclusion of a service in his former church, the Gospel Tabernacle, which became the Free Presbyterian Church in Ballymena and which is now named after him, Papa read from the back of his Bible a benedictory prayer. I remember watching him read it because reading prayers was something that I had only ever seen in school assembly – never in church. But Papa's speech deficiency was becoming more pronounced and he depended on reading. Until my grandfather died, he daily spent many hours reading the Bible. I am sure that as long as I live I will not have the privilege of knowing another person whose quiet but confident testimony depicts God's nature so apparently.

Nana Paisley died just over one year before Papa. She was a strong Scotch/Irish character, with all the zeal that comes with it. It was through a message spoken by her to a children's service that my father came to know Christ as his personal saviour. She had been considering the text concerning the Good Shepherd who gave his life for the sheep.

Nana's funeral was the first I had attended and so hers was the first corpse I ever saw. With natural trepidation I went into the room with Mum, Dad and Sharon. The ordeal was by no means a frightening one. Dad had explained to us previously that Nana's earthly body was in the coffin but her eternal life had already begun with Christ in heaven. She looked asleep. Her perfectly white hair crowned a face that had no anguish upon it. She was a nice-looking lady. It is strange and wonderful how children can accept things with an ease often lost to them in later age.

As children we saw more of our maternal grandparents because they lived only fifteen minutes' drive away from our house. Papa Cassells was small in height compared to Papa Paisley and he had dark brown eyes full of mischief! As he aged his sense of fun never waned. If I were to use one word to summarize him it would be the word 'upright'. He was a thoroughly good man. I knew as a youngster that I could never fib to Papa Cassells!

Papa had a grocer's shop and later a hardware business. It was he who supplied me with my first pair of stilts and he also mended my roller skates for me – the type that needed adjustments with a spanner. I used to listen for hours to him tell me stories all about the horse shows which he attended. I believe that it is important for children to love animals. There are few things I treasure as much as the time spent throughout my childhood and teenage years with my pets, and horseriding. Papa used to always be full of 'wee tips' on how to look after them and tricks to teach them.

Nana Cassells was as full of fun as Papa and had a reputation for her baking. Every Thursday afternoon, which was Papa's half-day off, they called and Nana brought a box with paper bags full of fresh soda, wheaten, potato bread; a cherry cake, and tucked into it a little parcel of her fudge – enough for five grandchildren. None of us ever had a birthday without being given an iced cake appropriately candled! Thankfully Mum inherited Nana's baking skills.

It was never hard for us to respect and love our grandparents. Our homes were cheered by their presence. Still their influence is strong. The constant support which we were given from them is a rare benefit for grandchildren to have a legacy of. Through times when adverse publicity was fierce and when it would have been convenient, even reasonable, for ageing grandparents to settle into retirement days aloof from what was happening with an air of 'I've done my bit' – through these times, with sincerity and enthusiasm, they encouraged Mum and Dad in what their convictions moved them to do.

They were the backdrop to our stage. Their share of disappointments and hardships was more than many will ever know.
The reign of Christ in them enabled them to prove personally
– and then pass on to us – that it is possible to go through
many waters without being drowned by the waves. I greatly
look forward to seeing them again.

Dad was raised to believe in the total lordship of Christ. A
lordship which built surface upon surface to create a relationship bonded and thoroughly secure in its two-way commitment. It meant total submission of self to Christ and to His
will – something which is not achieved in one fell swoop but
which comes with the development of a friendship as it moves
forward step by step. It is the outcome of both discipline and
love. As a boy, Dad found knowledge of salvation. As a man,
his ministry and political activities have been fair testing
grounds which have proved this lordship. The lordship of
Christ is a practical commodity, not just a spiritual ideal.

I get the impression that Dad's mother had more occasion
to discipline him than did his father; not that that is unusual
when the mother is not out working. I do not think Nana
Paisley was the type who would waste time before doling out
a punishment, nor did she use that familiar phrase, 'wait till
your father gets home'. It was instant – the back of the hair
brush on a bare bottom. Obviously this was effective, as you
could not find a man more docile than my Dad! Apparently
the above punishment was meted out for disobedience, cheek
and a few other things besides.

One prank of Dad's and his big brother Harold which
frequently concluded in this manner was the practice of rapping
on doors and taking off before the householder opened it in
response. Dad, being the younger, was unable to keep pace
with his brother and was usually the one delivered to his home
doorstep by an infuriated neighbour. Today, when Dad knocks
doors it is usually to ask for a vote and the infuriated response
is the exception, albeit more amusing.

Another activity well worth the 'hair brush treatment' was
when these two rascals held conversation with an elderly deaf
couple whom they would meet on their walk home from

school. This couple being members of my grandfather's congregation were much taken by the two boys and were no doubt flattered by their attention. The boys would strike up conversation;

'Good afternoon Mrs. X, and how are you today – still as deaf as ever?'

'I hope you haven't got on those red knickers again. It's time you put on clean ones.'

'The state of you yesterday was a disgrace, you 'awl mug.'

'Mr. X, how do you stick still being married to thon?'

To each statement (no doubt made with an innocent smile) the response was generous nods of approval and affectionate pats on the heads of their pastor's sons. How I would have enjoyed being witness should God have chosen to unstop the ears of this couple!

Auntie Margaret, the youngest in the family, must have endured much from these two. Dad seems to have been expert at assisting her down the stairs by using her pigtails as handle bars. Knowing Auntie Margaret, though, I reckon she could dose it out too!

An upbringing which permits dreams while supplying a channel through which to see those dreams realised is a good thing. Perhaps it is the key element in Dad's upbringing. I believe he had time to dream when a child and to express those dreams. With godly love, his parents moulded his childhood imagination to teach him what was attainable in life. The importance of the Sabbath in this process should never be underestimated – time for the Creator of Life. Today's pace of bringing up children is much more rapid. The soft mellowing of dream play into teenage ideals and then through to maturity is replaced with the harsh staccato beat of video, computer and television. The dream play is ready-made, teen ideals are pre-packed and maturity is gained by hard lessons where there is less than 'the daily recommended intake' of love to assuage the scarring.

It was Dad's childhood and teenage years which established and secured not only his faith, but also his loyalty to Ulster. I can understand how both of these have blended in his life.

Many view them as diverse. This is not so. They are perfectly engrafted – the proof is the fresh and plentiful fruit produced.

The shaping of Dad's political views came, it seems, from my grandfather's influence. Papa Paisley was a member of Lord Carson's Volunteer Force – Dad still has his old wooden training gun hanging in one of his offices. In 1912 Sir Edward Carson had founded the Ulster Volunteer Force to combat the Westminster Government's plans for Home Rule for the whole of Ireland. Although the 100,000-strong army started out with wooden guns, within two years they had assembled an arsenal of 24,000 rifles and three million rounds of ammunition. The UVF was one of the chief influences in the creation of Ulster, since it demonstrated that the Northern Protestants would fight rather than swap their links with Britain for rule by the Roman Catholic majority in Ireland.

My grandfather, then, was not the sort who left active service to others. As Dad was close to his father, the latter's political aspirations were bound to have an effect on him. I do not believe Dad followed his father's views blindly, but for a youngster the visual impact of political happenings is very strong. Things which I have seen in Ulster have compelled me more and drawn action from me which things simply taught would not have done. I do not see why this would differ in Dad's early life. It is evident that the Carson days have inspired my father's politics both in their values and in their tactics.

That is not to say that Dad views himself as another Carson however, I do not believe he does. The parallels drawn by political observers of my father's character and the events which surround him are strong, and yes, I agree there are similarities – but while this may be so it is not grounds for such a claim. Dad is a realist in his political outlook. He has learnt from example, which is to his credit as a statesman, but he has not forced a time-trap upon Ulster politics. Much of what he has done and continues to do has shattered the old Unionist embalmed corpse and replaced it with diversity, giving a choice to Unionists which hitherto did not exist. It has been an uphill struggle and it is all too easy for those who have failed to win a political platform to criticize my father's career. Were his motivation merely to be 'another Carson' his task would have been a good deal simpler – he would have been engaged in fitting the mould, not breaking it.

I believe Dad's motivations to get involved come from a pastor's heart, and not from a desire to achieve some self-centred, ego-fulfilling ambition. That he encouraged Mum to run for election before he was ever involved himself evidences his lack of personal aspirations as a political hero. Once I asked Dad directly:

'Dad, why did you ever get into politics?'

'The call of the people,' he replied simply without even a pause to think.

Strange as it may seem to political analysts, to historians and to sceptics, I honestly believe the matter was and still is that straight-forward to my father. His love and his respect for the people he serves are his motivation. Sometimes I truly wish that people would have the sense enough to take things as they are on the surface instead of reading deep philosophical reasons between the lines.

I too have had people speculating on my motives. I did a painting once entitled 'Homage to Huddleston'. In a review of the exhibition, a reporter claimed, 'Miss Paisley's art obviously reflects her religious upbringing'. He expanded this by using 'Homage' as a typical example, saying it was a work cynically named after Father Huddleston, a priest with whom my father had been in public debate many years before. The colours in their brilliance and the texture of the work reflected my 'hatred'.

Had the reporter taken the time, I could have told him the true story behind that piece. I had been painting a little landscape which went wrong and had literally scribbled over it. It looked quite attractive and for a joke I framed it up, naming it 'Homage to Huddleston' especially for my brother-in-law, John Huddleston, who hates abstract art! Talk about reading between the lines! I'm afraid our lives are always under magnifying glasses – too bad the users have such squints!

Papa Paisley did not leave to others the task of teaching his children about their heritage, either. It seems that religious convictions were the basis of his appreciation for the political liberty enjoyed as part of the British empire. The history of the martyrs and the covenanters was woven as thoroughly into Dad's childhood teaching as the lives of the Prophets. The sacrifices of time, ambition, and often life in order to maintain liberty and Protestantism were established in my father's thinking just as carefully as were cleanliness and polite manners. Some of Dad's earliest memories include leafing through such texts as *Foxe's Book of Martyrs* and the *History of Protestantism* to look at the pictures – I presume this was when he had been sent to my grandfather's study to do penance for annoying the neighbours or talking to the deaf!

The ideals and values behind politics are of the utmost importance to a party, for it is these which mould its politicians and which in times of opposition hold the party together. In Ulster's case it is a good thing that it is these values which matter most to Dad. Ulster holds a place in his heart, unseen by the human eye, but proved by his faithful years of unwavering and unselfish service.

We are all products of our upbringing. The strongest line in my father's traces happiness. I am glad mine does too and its strong brightness dims into insignificance the more melancholy, sombre lines woven by Ulster's troubles. My brother Kyle, giving his testimony one day at an open-air meeting, took the theme of upbringing. He referred his listeners to their different upbringings, and then told them he had the greatest upbringing of them all. Not because of his family, but because Christ had brought him up out of a pit of fear and from the miry clay of discomfort and confusion and had placed his feet upon a rock, establishing a new way for him.

This well summarizes the upbringing which was of most importance to Dad's parents as they raised him. My own parents in turn have laid no less importance upon the same in raising their own children. I cannot help but marvel at the manner – the extent and the mercy – of the love that God has bestowed on us to enable us to be called his children, the children of the Resurrection. With age and experience comes acceptance that not all your aspirations are realistic ones.

Circumstances over which you have no control or influence can bring to a close, or even abruptly end those aspirations. My upbringing has taught me not to cling too tightly to anything in this world but to set my affection upon my Father's God.

CHAPTER THREE

How Now Brown School

I was listening to Radio Ulster one day as a retiring B.B.C. Controller General was being interviewed. He was reminiscing about the changes which had taken place since he took up the job. One matter was that of the 'B.B.C. accent' and he was rabbiting on about the change in this area away from the 'very awfully' pronunciation that was once the only acceptable form. The 'how now brown school', he said, was no longer the norm for the B.B.C. 'How now brown school' as opposed to 'how now brown cow' – struck me as very funny and an apt title for this chapter. 'Brown school' describes my schooldays perfectly. Actually we were all clad in bottle-green uniforms, but the staidness of rules was as brown as the stickiest mud.

Education provides a dilemma in Northern Ireland. There is the whole debate of integrated education which I believe is part of the solution for our Province. Religion has no place in this, however. The greatest curse to religious persuasion is when it is brought into the classrooms of State schools and a prayer and a hymn at the beginning of a school day gives a false image of religion.

The responsibility for religious education lies with the church and the home. Under the State system, any church has the right to establish its own independent schools and parents who opt to send their children to such a school are therefore well aware of exactly the religious doctrines their offspring are taught. State schools in Ulster have come to be regarded as

Protestant schools because of the number of clergy given a place on their Boards – a throwback from when the schools had been set up by the Church.

What further muddies the water of integrated education at the moment is the middle-class 'hands-across-the-great-divide' clique and their efforts made in the guise of it. The Government is blindly prepared to hand out cash to promote such efforts and does not seem to realise that it is shooting its own ideal in the foot – but then it is not uncommon for the Government to ignore advice and opinions from those whom their policies affect.

My own education was a rare enough conglomeration. An all-girls school from Primary I to Upper VI, taking me from the ages of four to seventeen, followed by four years at university – an American establishment independent of such educational legislation. The first time I ever was in a mixed class – male and female I mean – was my first lecture at university. As a result I do have strong views against all-girl or all-boy schools, and I am also a supporter of integrated education in Ulster for the State schools – provided, as I say, that no religious education or services are held. I suppose religion could be treated as a comparative studies course, but even that I would think wiser to avoid. If some organisation or church desired to have their own school, they could have it and raise their own funds for it and teach whatever they liked.

Frankly I could not see myself sending my child, if ever I had one, to that type of independent school. Christian education often only gives parents the excuse of abdicating their responsibility for spiritual instruction and leaving it in the hands of the school, thus risking the danger of a generation of spiritual cripples.

Dad's attitude to school was always refreshing. He was particularly interested in history lessons and R.E. lessons.

'Well, what rubbish is that old Methodist minister telling you?' he would say in jest. I'd give him a run-down of the lessons (what I could recall) and Dad would either re-teach them if he was in a more serious mood, or give a great 'Huh!' accompanied by a laugh and go on his way. I remember once while I was nearing my 'A' level exams, Dad came in and lifted one of my history text books. It was on Irish history and I was in the middle of preparing notes for an essay. He flipped through it.

'Is that what they are teaching you?' and tut-tutted with disgust. About fifteen minutes later he came back with an armful of Irish history books. 'There you are, dear,' he said, clattering the pile onto the desk, 'read those if you want to know Irish history.' I looked at the pile, looked at him, and said, 'Thanks,' and we both grinned. My poor history teacher was demented as a result of all my questions.

School was important to my parents, but it was never over-important. Some parents were hyper – always bringing the headmistress bunches of flowers, dressed to kill at sports day, 'my Stephanie this' and 'my Claire that' – total headcases, but extremely amusing nonetheless. Many a mizzley sports day was brightened listening to two pink-lipsticked mothers engaged in oh-so-polite conversation on their respective daughters' merits, all the while cutting tripe out of each other!

I never was very keen on school and always found it depressing when the end of the holidays demanded the return of a wearisome timetable to dictate the spending of precious hours. I admit that I did enter very whole-heartedly into 'messing about' and that detention for being late was a weekly addition to my schedule. My parents never got too worked up about punishments. They reckoned that they had been earned, and they were perfectly correct! There were, however, times when Dad was angry about situations and the Board of Governors were the recipients of his letters and the headmistress of his wrath. These did, in retrospect, warm my heart, as did such outbursts from friends' parents, but at the instant of delivery knees knocked feverishly beneath gym skirts. Our headmistress was a small woman and the usual nicknames were breathed throughout the corridors: 'Big E' and 'Evil Ethel' when she was out of favour and 'wee Miss Gray' when she was in. I'm sure she won't be offended at being mentioned, for since leaving school I have met her on several occasions. She was known mostly, I suppose, for her rigorous discipline, and when our paths crossed again, I have to admit I wondered if my hair was neat and my skirt the correct length, if I was slouching and if my grammar was proper. Then I thought, 'Stuff that!' and was perfectly at ease in her company.

It was rare that Dad made it to any school event and when he did there was always a bit of 'fuss'. In my early teenage days, awkward embarrassment would pour itself all over me, but then it was no different for my friends when *their* parents were around either, and thirteen soon turned to fourteen, bringing with it an ability to handle such situations more confidently.

One school event that Dad always supported was the annual pantomime. It was held in the week approaching Christmas, just before the holidays began. The grand finale of the events included a Sixth Form skit on the staff (and then the staff themselves came on stage to get their own back). One year the members of staff for which I and two friends were responsible were the three Methodist ministers who taught in the school.

We based our skit on the then popular TV series 'The Goodies' (the name was appropriate for obvious reasons) and as they were also a trio, it suited perfectly. I was able to get hold of three dog collars and the other gear that goes with the job. We brightened the sombre outfits by adding silver wings and halos and came on stage tandem style, freaking out to the tune of the real Goodies' current hit 'The Funky Gibbon' only with more appropriate words: 'Do, do, do the Methodist Movement . . .' Unfortunately, one of the wives of these men saw cause for offence – all the others were highly amused by it. It was her reason that was really amusing to us. She was convinced that Dad had put me up to writing this to 'get at' the Methodists! I've yet to see Dad have time to write a panto script for a Sixth Former! The fact of the matter is that I wouldn't for the life of me have shown Dad the script for he would have forbidden me to submit it!

The most joyous benefit of school life is the friendships that remain over the years. I was blessed with great friends at school; in fact, that is what made school tolerable for me! My closest friend was a girl called Jill. We had a friendship which spanned from our primary school years until the day we left on completion of 'A' levels, and we still maintain contact with one another.

We spent long hours poring over homework, quizzing each other, discussing topics, and laughing at our various solutions to the difficulties of world history. We both took the same subjects for 'A' level, but it was in art that most of our time was spent.

In our earlier years at school, animals were our great passion and we were intent upon becoming vets until we found out that Latin was required. Our Latin classes were disastrous. We had a kindly soul of a teacher, but whatever she did she could not quite capture the attention of 3B. Part of the reason for this was that we had her class before swimming on a Friday morning. To us that was the weekend! Without fail, we would race to see who could get their swimsuit on undetected before the class was up.

Third year must be the bane of every teacher's life. The thrill of flouting authority is a challenge. Childhood years are ending; adulthood is opening. It is wanted; yet unwanted. Rules are described by words like 'silly' and 'boring'. Teachers are 'prudes' and the future is no further than finding an excuse for not having a certain piece of homework done. Hockey matches are of prime importance in a day's timetable, and stealing plums from the trees behind the netball court is the most important matter for consideration through morning Maths classes! Tripping senior girls as they race along corridors to be in class before the bell must be the object of every Third Former I have ever known!

Our school had many rules that were an absolute blast to disregard. Everybody had to go outside during ten-minute morning break. We had the type of cloakroom lockers made of wire, known by us as 'the cages', which were easy for teachers to inspect and very hard to hide in. Jill and I came up with what proved to be a very successful way to hide in these 'cages'. You simply held on to two coat hooks, placed your feet on the heavy cross bar (which ran along at the level the coats hung down to) and pulled the Burberrys over you. This was fine until a certain rather large Maths teacher was on duty. There was no love lost between us and from that day, never a chance of any being found.

Just at the worst possible moment for us, the cage broke from its fixture, flipping me forward like a catapult onto the floor and swallowing Jill's body like a laundry chute – but catching her feet which ended up inches from the teacher's nose.

Then came the rage. This was an act of 'Gad' as she called him. 'Be sure your sin will find you out,' she preached, her plump finger flailing the air of the dim cloakrooms. We were dragged to her room and given a list of equations for extra homework and told that we would be in for detention (that meant more Maths)! Our fathers would be most angry, she told us 'sneaky disobedient wee girls'. Truth of the matter was that our fathers would and did have a good laugh with us over the incident.

I am quite sure that my father was as big a prankster as anyone else at school because, although not forthcoming with his own mischiefs (no doubt so that we couldn't 'cast them up' at an inconvenient moment), he was always having a laugh with us about the things we got up to for jokes at school. At school and throughout my university years I learnt about life as much through pranks as through serious discussion.

My father was always very strict about family worship and still is. During our schooldays this was always carried out first thing in the morning. Sometimes if we were going to be late we would only have a Bible reading and only Dad would pray, meaning that in the car between home and school, each of us would have to take our turn to pray. Sharon always sat in the front with Mum driving and the other four of us were in the back. Sharon prayed first, and then we prayed, in order of age. One morning Sharon was praying and I'm afraid I wasn't being attentive; in fact, you could say I was in another world. I was looking out of the window and began singing a little jingle that was running through my head. It was from an advertisement for chicken – hardly the most spiritual thing to sing during prayer; 'Moy Park chicken, tender tasty chicken, tenderest, tastiest chicken in the world . . . bet you never saw a chicken play a banjo before'. There was utter silence and how Sharon managed to get her head turned in such an angle to look in amazement at me, who sat directly behind her, is more than I shall ever know!

'Rhonda!' said Mum. To be honest, I was just as amazed for I wasn't aware of what I was doing at all. The prayer session was blown because we all laughed the rest of the journey to school.

On another occasion when prayer was being said, Ian and Kyle got into a squabble on the back seat. Trying to bring the situation into control, Mum looked back. Meanwhile, the driver in front stopped suddenly, Mum looked round, braked, but too late – bump! Fortunately, we were in a rush-hour crawl so there was little damage and no injuries. The driver of the other car was in a hot temper as he jumped out and came storming to Mum.

'What way's that to drive?' he growled. 'Oh, Mrs Paisley!' he continued, now in more of a hoarse growl, 'it's a good job nobody was hurt,' regaining himself after the initial shock of realising he had just snapped the head off a certain clergyman's wife! 'I'm a policeman, you know, and that was careless driving. What were you doing?'

'Praying,' said Mum, before he could get another word of his lecture delivered. Well, if he looked shocked the first time, he was flabbergasted this time! These two instances of prayer times in the car were exceptions rather than the rule, otherwise none of us would be around to tell the tale!

At the age of 16, I attended a conference in Edinburgh, Scotland. The theme of the week was printed boldly on a banner over the platform. It read, 'To obey is better than sacrifice'. Seeing those words for some part of a day for five days of a week had to do something to my brain.

The message to the church body on earth was clear and straightforward enough but its relevance to me as an individual I didn't really see at all at first. By the time the week was over, that had changed! God wanted obedience from me as his child. His blood had redeemed me and assured me of eternal life with him, something which would not alter, but was I going to be content with that for my life? Possibly obedience would lead my life off in a completely different direction than I would choose. Would I obey even if that were the case? The timing for such considerations was right. I was entering my 'A' level year and would have to decide what I intended to do regarding a career of some sort. Art college was what I was aiming at, but as Ulster boasts only one such institution, I knew I'd best have a few other options.

Dad had previously suggested to me that I think about applying to Bob Jones' University in the USA. During my father's first imprisonment, Bob Jones' University gave him an honorary Doctorate of Divinity. The friendship of the university and in particular of the Jones family is precious not just to us as a family, but to the Free Presbyterian Church. It was not a popular move for Dr Bob to associate himself with a jail bird, but such considerations don't mean anything when defence of the truth is the issue at stake.

It would be an experience of a lifetime to study in America and the University offered a degree in Fine Art. Also, I would be able to take courses in the Bible, which would not be available elsewhere.

Four years in America was as daunting as it was appealing. Four years was quite some time to be away from home and to be there without school friends of many years – of these things I wasn't sure! My closest friend Jill, was aiming at art college too: it would have been pleasant to have continued with our studies together. She and I were 'soul mates' since our very first year at school and fourteen years is a long time. Now I was questioning what I had thought my direction was and I was no longer quite as certain as I had been. The previous Easter at our Church's Annual Convention I had made a commitment to Christ concerning my life. I had responded to an appeal to youth made by my father for those of us who were saved to place our lives at God's disposal so that if he directed us to a full-time ministry for him we would be willing, and likewise, if he directed us to any other occupation, we would be willing. Certainly it was a reasonable commitment to be simply willing to let God choose your future. His choice, I knew, would make considerably more sense than mine. At this conference I was being reminded of my commitment, and 'letting go' wasn't proving to be the easiest thing I'd ever done.

That June I finished my Lower Sixth term. September began my final year at school and with it 'A' level examinations. I was turned down in my interview and applications for the Art College in Ulster, but was accepted by the Bob Jones' University, provided I achieved the necessary 'A' level grades. 'To obey is better than sacrifice' didn't feel too hot a theory for life when I found myself at the other side of the Atlantic, sharing a room with girls who at first could hardly make sense of my accent and who were of the opinion that I had escaped from a country where you walked down the street ducking the bullets! I learnt a lesson in those first few weeks of university life which has stuck with me since – that work is the best remedy for lonesomeness, for defeat, for failure and for anything else that comes along. I have had many instances since, when work has proved itself to be my dearest companion and the only medicine worthwile taking. Let me assure you this is quite a different view of work than the 'Presbyterian work ethic'!

University days broadened and deepened my appreciation of home life. Living with girls from all sorts of backgrounds, being away totally from family influence as far as daily and routine decisions went, cemented my views on what the home is all about. I dated a guy for quite some time whose background was as good as opposite from my own. We had many things in common, but our basis for them stemmed from completely different reasons. Take art, for example. It was my joy because in it I had found a total privacy away from being 'the daughter of . . .' He had found the same privacy but for him it was because he was the only person in his home who believed in Christ as Saviour. We understood and shared the intimacy between the painter and his work, having learnt it within our vastly different experiences.

We both loved long walks and spent hours, often in silence, walking and sharing the wealth of nature's solace when political storms dragged through my brain, uprooting hope and devastating trust. His came from needing that converse to settle trust again also, and to water the seeds of hope, but not because politics raged in his land, but because his father's problem with drink tore asunder his home life. We both shared the quietness and assuaging peace of walking even though we seemed to have started our trek at different sides of the forest.

We loved the sky and the stars. We played games with their patterns and the moon was our common focal point wherever we went and when we separated because of holidays or work. That was something we built together and it united our lives which often seemed so incompatible as far as others went. We faced the odds and won, because we had learnt that others came second when it came to deciding matters of permanence in life. Our homes were cherished, and we pitied friends whose homes didn't mean a toss to them. When circumstances sent us on our different ways, we finally parted company as far as geography goes, but we each took from those years of friendship and understanding a new dimension of life previously untapped, simply because in our homes we had learnt to love the family bond, ideal or not as far as circumstances or others' opinions went.

Brown school days were no longer the mode when university life opened its door. My years at Bob Jones' University were thoroughly enjoyable, often packed with laughter despite the sheer hard work. The schedule was rigorous, the University concentrated its efforts in character development as much as on education. There was a daily required meeting of the student body at 11 a.m. No lectures were held at that hour so there was no excuse! It was a devotional time. Necessary announcements were made, the University creed was repeated, a hymn sung and then about thirty minutes was given to the speaker. Usually this was Dr Jones III, Present of the university, or Dr Jones Jr., Chancellor.

This hour was purposed to build a unity between student body and faculty, to create an aspect of a family in the university – a rare thing in today's education, possibly not done anywhere in Great Britain. But it was a thing which I, for most of the time, enjoyed. Dr Jones Jr. simply chatted away to us, totally informally, just as though there were only twenty or thirty in attendance, not 6,000! He loved to make wee digs at the Science Department, and he took what chances he got to stir the Bible Faculty also! But it was all in good humour and after his messages, there was always something which stimulated thought to keep your mind going for the rest of the day. He spoke with complete ease but never failed to hit the nail on the head!

'To obey is better than sacrifice' has appeared many times to me to be a contradiction in terms. Obedience itself often would seem like the sacrifice rather than the better option, but appearances aren't always what they seem, thank goodness. For example, it appeared that my father's imprisonments would be the worst possible thing that could happen regarding our Church. It turned out they greatly inspired our people and developed them spiritually in a relatively brief period time, to a degree which would have taken years of preaching and exhortation, Dad often says.

My father has no regrets concerning his imprisonments nor any other aspect of his religious and political work. He has taught us never to regret nor try and retrieve what you have given to or for others. If we love and do not achieve or gain what we had dearly hoped such love would win, we ought not to bury ourselves in regret and defeat. Having given, be content to let it remain a bright and happy gift. Learn and be thankful for its lessons, using them to live with greater discernment and continue as kindly as if you had succeeded. Watching Dad permit the absorbtion of gentleness into his life through adverse circumstances has drawn from him a calm walk whatever storm is currently raging and the destructive spirit of bitterness has not reigned in his life nor our home as a result. This is my father's choice in obedience and living and while he has passed on to us his children their principles he recognizes that we must choose our own way in life.

CHAPTER FOUR

The Troubles

For a child, things of great consequence always have a beginning and an end. 'The troubles' began, to my mind as a child, one morning when I learned that the Rt. Hon. Bill Craig, then Minister of Home Affairs, had been sacked by the Northern Irish Prime Minister, Captain Terence O'Neill. It was the late '60s and O'Neill, a liberal Unionist, had been pursuing a policy of appeasement with the Roman Catholics. Up to that moment, Bill Craig had been the most outspoken defender of Protestant rights in the Unionist Party. After his sacking, he founded his own (short-lived) party and the opposition to O'Neill moved out of Stormont and onto the streets.

On that first morning I was sitting in my parent's bedroom on a little red leather chair. The sun was making chequered designs on the carpet. As it entered the room its light was broken by the wire protective grids over the glass. Mum was making the bed and talking to the babysitter about the news.

'Such a move was sure to cause trouble,' I heard her say. I remember feeling frightened because of Dad's involvement in things.

That day for me was when 'the troubles' began. Regrettably, my childhood brought no memory which signalled an end to this event of such consequence. Not long ago I saw Bill Craig again, whom I had not seen for many years. He was walking his dog along the shore late on a Sunday afternoon. I wished that seeing him signified the end of the 'the troubles'. Then I laughed at my stupidity and continued my dander. 'The troubles' have been a way of life for my generation. With them came both my parents' public involvement as political representatives – more so, of course, Dad's. I suppose they have made us what we are because the dimension created in our lives and the direction dictated by them over which we are helpless would otherwise not have existed. It is a dimension we would gladly do without. It is none the less one that we have to accept, and it will influence us forever even when its era concludes.

The first political slogan that I recall chorusing with heartfelt belief was 'O'Neill must go'. Heartfelt, I admit, only because to my young mind, O'Neill was the man whom I held responsible for putting my father in jail. Would that political reasoning remained so straightforward! Eventually, in 1969, Terence O'Neill did go, but not without leaving a considerable trail of political débris behind, the aftermath of which Ulster is still suffering.

Dad's first imprisonment was in 1966; the sentence was for three months. Sharon, Cherith and I were the only children then and the details of the Court proceedings really are very vague, but the atmosphere is vivid. People were angry and the church was disheartened although one hundred percent behind Dad in support of his stand. I became aware that people knew who my father was and also that many hated him. But I could see that many admired him and knew him to be 'doing what was right'. 'Doing what was right' was a phrase that I heard over and over again from people who would stop my mother when we were shopping or out somewhere. They would thank her for Dad, saying that he was 'doing what was right'. Funnily, I would use that expression when I couldn't explain to my friends exactly what he was doing!

Dad's arrest came after a Free Church march to picket the Irish Presbyterian Assembly. Although the marchers themselves were attacked by Republican Catholics, it was Dad and two other ministers, Ivan Foster and John Wylie, who were charged with public order offences. All three declared their innocence and refused to be bound over to keep the peace for two years. The result was three months inside Crumlin Road Prison. My mother was full of inventiveness in order to keep our minds lifted away from the hardness of the experience. I am sure that it helped Mum too, to have three young responsibilities to concentrate on!

We visited Dad all together. The cell we met in was a small room. We were taken first to the waiting room which I recall as having a lot of wood. There was a tall glass display case which contained things the prisoners made and the prices of them. There were little buildings made from matchsticks which were amazing to look at. Then we would be taken into the visiting room. It was completely bare with a door on each side and a table that ran solidly across from one wall to the next. The doors had square windows. We would wait and hear Dad coming. A man in uniform led him in. The warders were first very nice but Sharon and I always felt frightened of them. They had power to keep Dad, so naturally it was with awe that we thought of them. Cherith was only a baby and she would crawl between Mum and Dad across the table. Mum lifted us up to kiss Dad but for the rest of the time we had to stand beside her. The warden watched through the door. I most hated watching the large gates of the prison being shut as we left and my greatest fear was that the prison would go on fire and Dad would be trapped.

The second imprisonment came in 1969. Once again, Dad was charged with organising a demonstration to protest against O'Neill's policies. Violence had broken out, and although Dad is always quick to condemn violence from any quarter, he was the main organiser of the demonstration and therefore was held responsible.

My memories of this time are clearer. Dad explained to Sharon and me that he would probably be taken to prison again. I remember Sharon really sobbing and her hanky became so wet I gave her mine. I have to admit that I really hated the policeman who eventually came to arrest Dad. I don't hate the man now and I have never felt that type of animosity towards anyone since, but it makes me realise the strength of feeling that can be aroused in a child.

Being three years older now, Sharon and I could comprehend the situation more. Mum wisely turned our attention to 'the three wee ones' as we called Cherith, Kyle and Ian. We were not to let them see our fears, for they would be missing Dad. We had come through before and would do so again. But it was hard.

The arrest was clumsy. The police broke down the glass door of our entrance porch. Dad's hand was badly cut. Crowds of supporters gathered at the gates. The press were everywhere. The first sentence was for three months, but at the appeal it was changed to five months! Dad was back in prison.

Visits this time were in a large long room, the walk to which seemed endless. Families were all brought in first and each one placed at the narrow end of the long tables. The prisoners were then marched in and, to orders, were dismissed to sit at the other end of the table. To my young mind the table looked a mile long. This time we could not even touch Dad and he was in a brown uniform with a red star on his shoulder, and a number.

A warden sat on a little platform watching everything and two others walked up and down, up and down the whole time. This time I really tried to understand all about why Dad was in prison – and can recall one day thinking that I could never understand it. I suppose my child's mind had wearied itself out and given up.

Naturally my father's two imprisonments left deep impressions on each of us. Perhaps they are the most potent lessons experienced in our childhood. As children our calendar became dated by these two events. Something happened while, before or after Dad was in prison the first time or the second time! We used to get looks of horror from people when we said that. One year, when we were on a caravan holiday, Sharon and I were playing with another wee girl we had met. We were all on swings in the park area and whatever we were jabbering about had got Sharon and me into a lengthy discussion as to whether it had been when Dad was in jail the first or second time. The wee girl joined in:

'Has your Da' been in twice? Mine's only been in once. His was for breakin' an' ent'rin'. What did yours do?'

'He was doing what was right,' was the stereo reply.

'Nobody does what's right in prison.'

'Well, Daddy did,' said Sharon, in such a voice of defiance that the wee girl just said 'Oh!'

Upon arriving back at the caravan for tea I asked Mum 'What's breakin' an' ent'rin'?' I had to repeat it a few times for to me it was all one word! Eventually she caught on. 'It's breaking and entering,' she explained. 'Where did you hear that?' We told her and how she laughed before telling us what the crime was!

One evening during Dad's second imprisonment, Mum was putting Ian and Kyle to bed and each were saying their prayers. Kyle had said his first and it was Ian's turn. He wanted Mum to stay with him longer than his prayers would last and had devised a little plan. He would say the first couple of lines of his prayers and then say, 'No more prayers'. So Mum would say, 'Finish your prayers, Ian,' and then he would start again, only to announce almost immediately, 'No more prayers.' After a couple of times Mum called his bluff. 'All right, Ian, this is the last time.' So he began: 'God b'ss Daddy in prison, God b'ss Mummy, God b'ss Kyle and Cherith and Rhonda and Sharon, and' (opening his screwed up eyes just slightly so as not to miss the reaction) 'God b'ss O'Neill, ha! ha! ha!' What could a mother do but laugh?

This was the time Dad became seriously involved in politics. On his release from prison one of his first acts was to stand as a candidate against O'Neill. He lost, but in the following year, after O'Neill had been forced to resign, Dad defeated his successor and entered Stormont. That same year, 1970, Dad won a seat at Westminster. Since then we have had a father who is both a minister and an MP.

As I said at the beginning, this book does not pretend to be a proper biography. I will not attempt to follow the twists of Northern Irish politics through the last eighteen years – the hopes, the disappointments, the betrayals, and always, it seems, the long hard struggle. And in the thick of it all – my father.

Perhaps, though, it will be these last three years fighting the Anglo-Irish Agreement that will prove to be in history the most truthful memorial of the character and manner of my father. The thoughts of the people of Ulster will be written forever in these times, for out of them will come the direction of our future.

The Agreement was signed in November 1985 by the Westminster and Dublin governments. It attempts to forge closer links between Ulster and the Irish Republic – but could only do that by ignoring the views of the majority of people in Ulster.

The protest campaign against the Agreement has either cemented people's loyalty to the Unionist leadership or else it has driven them away from the elected leaders and towards various factions which have sprung up in reaction to it. None of these reactions has so far achieved anything like the permanency or impact of the Joint Unionist campaign carried out by the leaders of the Official Unionist Party and the Democratic Unionist Party – Jim Molyneaux and my father. Their method has been greatly criticised – they have not been tough enough for some, they have been too tough for others. They have not laid enough cards publicly on the table others have claimed, their leadership lacks forthrightness according to yet another group. Members of both parties have resigned in the thick of the battle, some of whom had seemed made of stronger stuff before the crisis came about. All this criticism and division is a hard pill to swallow when on the home front you are aware of the mammoth efforts, care, consideration and the sheer workload the leadership has demanded.

In this I know Dad is taking what he sees to be a path of obedience. Obedience not just to himself and his conscience on the matter but also to those who have put their trust in his leadership by voting for him. That is a sacred trust between him and his people on which he will not move. If the people at the end of the day, choose via the ballot box a way other than the one he will offer should negotiations succeed, then he will accept it. I would be a liar to claim that there are no moments of doubt in my mind regarding Ulster's future, and

I certainly do not have the same security of belief that my
father has concerning the same.

At the beginning of any conflict there is usually a tremendous
sense of comradeship and even excitement. People unite against
a common enemy. Everyone is keen to pool resources and all
have 'fight' in their veins. In the long days that follow when
the fight becomes a drag the memory of the comradeship and
the initial warcry are often the only lifeline to hope that
survives. The first rally arranged against the signing of the
Anglo-Irish Agreement was a breathtaking event. The day
favoured us with sunshine and brightness, and the people
responded to the call to come to the City Hall, Belfast. In
coming they were indicating their opposition to the Agreement. Theirs was a lawful and undeniable 'No'.

Dad was in a quiet but tense mood at home that morning.
He believed that the rally would be a success because if it were
not, he said, the people knew that Ulster's cause was finished.
Dad is a politician, and almost the only one I know who, in a
consistent way, gives the people credibility. His view is that
the man in the street 'knows and can be depended upon'.
Individuals have and will let him down, but on the whole, his
people have proved dependable. Most other politicians, in
whose presence I have been, have much less respect and trust
in the people. They talk as though political involvement has
given them a rare insight into life – they themselves have the
knowledge and know-how but anyone else? Well, they are just
gullible creatures, these 'men in the street'. Such politicians
seem to think that being elected to some wee petty council,
robbed of any significant power by a retarded British Government, has brought them an almighty gift of wisdom. Would
to God that it had! And they treat the man in the street as a
wandering imbecile awaiting their instructions.

Ian, Kyle, Cherith and I left home before Mum and Dad, as
we were all helping with various bits and pieces. My car was
loaded with picket boards we had hammered up. There were
buckets for 'Ulster Fund' collections, rolls of stickers reading
'Ulster Says No' for distribution, Ulster flags and Union Jacks

stuck out everywhere and all had to be delivered according to Dad's instructions. There was hardly room for us to pile in.

The next time I saw Dad was as he and Jim Molyneaux led the MPs onto the huge scaffold platform. There was such resolve written on his face I knew that it marked the beginning of a long hard task. Many people seemed to think this Agreement would crumble without any demands being made upon them. Somehow I felt very aware that the warnings of the leaders that this would not be so would only be accepted when proved by time.

Along with various of the Ulster MPs, their wives, families and organisers of the rally, I joined the single file procession inside to climb to the top of the City Hall's dome and look at the gathering masses. It was like a lesson in pointilism. The crowds threw out their colour in a vast span along the streets – speckled and bright, little dots on a living canvas. Buildings looked docile beside this wealth of life, their architecture quietly submitting in its inability to compete. Returning to be one of the touches of colour in this spectrum, I stood listening to the voice of Unionism and watching the MPs step forward in turn to sign their pledge against the Agreement. The crowd roared. The power of the cause, its compelling aura, its urgency and its necessity crackled through the crisp November air. There was an undeniable sense of festivity, the sort of hype that you feel in your stomach. It was strange to be aware of two such opposite sensations in body and soul – the sombreness and the elation balanced each other.

A year passed and again the City Hall was the rallying point for the first anniversary protest of the signing of the Agreement. The year had cleared the decks of many who disagreed with the methods used to protest. Council work in the Province was in disarray. A day of action had brought Ulster to a standstill. The Secretary of State and other Northern Ireland ministers were hounded everywhere they went. Anger and resentment were constantly in evidence. The Unionist MPs had resigned in protest, fought the by-elections on the Agreement issue and had been re-elected, bar one, whose seat was in a borderline constituency. Clubs and organisations sprouted up everywhere, some of which had already died without leaving any seed to follow. The Elected Assembly was closed down, leaving nothing between council level and MP representation. Violence and deaths increased. The Irish Republic, a foreign power, began to interfere in Ulster's business, and all with the blessing of the British Government. It was a long year. My father was busier than ever – and that's saying something!

This time the crowd had increased in number. It was considerably larger and looking again from the lofty vantage point of the dome the difference was evident. The determination of the previous year was still there, but the resentment was more profound. The frustration of Ulster presently is that over-government has rendered us helpless. The negative stance of consecutive British Governments with all their restrictive measures is in direct contrast to the spirit of Ulster Protestantism.

At this second rally I still found a degree of comradeship among the people. Time was proving the leadership right when they said that this Agreement would not disappear overnight. The sustaining factor for Dad through all these months of division within the ranks, and debauchery without, has been his cheerful heart as he has carried out the daily tasks that fall to his hand.

Meanwhile, in the midst of this struggle the political landscape of Ulster is changing. The ideals, the 'isms', which motivated my father's generation – Loyalism, Orangeism and Unionism – have different meanings for mine. The 'isms' of youth were bathed in a soft blue tenderness for my father, like the light a full moon casts through tall forest trees, making the green mossy paths take on a clear, luminous quality. That inviting appearance is from a past night now. The 'isms' of Ulster have been lost in the gathering darkness of terrorism and their pathway has been obscured to my generation because the will to win what is in reality a war has not existed. My peers have had to feel their way through the forest, and have had to watch death upon death, sorrow upon sorrow, as they scratch out a new path for Ulster's future.

Loyalism has been redefined. I think loyalty first means

loyalty to those who have lost loved ones and to those who live maimed for life because of some atrocity. It does not pull from me a grand idea of faithfulness to the British link. It makes me desire to fight betrayal because its cost has been loss of life and fullness of health for so many of our people. Ironically, Loyalism has become anti-Government, since governing Ulster has been a long line of Secretaries of State who can never excel in any of their personal abilities because their policy prevents any progress.

Orangeism lost its purity and had become a voting machine for the Official Unionist Party. Its leaders were political appointees aided and abetted by ecumencial chaplains who had already given up their faith in Protestant principles. Backing of the leadership of Terence O'Neil and the institution's attacks through resolutions on my father and his supporters early disillusioned me to the effectiveness of this once important body in Ulster's affairs. Disillusionment has not yet given birth to the militancy which some would claim exists lower down the ranks of the order today among the young. I never have, to be honest, thought much of the Orange Order. I respect and would defend their right to exist and to parade till they were blue in the face if they so desired. But the orange sashes and King Billy's white horse that decks many a fluttering banner makes me turn in disgust when I see how weak-minded and feeble-kneed and self-seeking some of the bowler-hatted, white-gloved 'leaders' among them turn out to be.

The greatest 'ism', Unionism itself, is a much more fragmented thing than it was in my father's youth. There is thankfully not the same adherence to 'British is Best' that there used to be. The close ties with Conservatism have separated like a yolk from its white, and I doubt there will ever arise in Ulster another generation that will desire to see them scrambled again. The 'isms' for my generation have never had the opportunity to envelop us in their hope. This is because they have been distorted by insensitive government – and tried by the bomb and the bullet. We are therefore abandoning many of the ill-founded hopes, and creating a new purity which has at its heart a determination to frustrate terrorism, however long the war

lasts. This is precisely why talking with, co-operation with and
working with the representatives of terrorism – i.e. IRA Sinn
Fein – is so unacceptable to those in Ulster who seek the best
for her future.

CHAPTER FIVE

The Rhythm of Ulster

To know a person, that is to know them genuinely and not just be acquainted with them, you must understand their heart. It is a process which takes time. To know Ulster and comprehend the situation here you must understand the beat of the land and the rhythm of its music. It is a process which takes time. Outsiders do not usually give the time. They rush in with a camera crew, scan the scenery, comment on the deaths and the immovable position of both 'sides' as they put it, and they are gone. The world is no clearer for their comment and Ulster no richer for their visit.

Often I have sat alone on a hillside close to the beach which I love to walk along and tried to take in, to absorb into my being the beauty of this land. Sometimes it is a clear sky that lightens overhead, pouring coolness over the trees and stretching out the calm waters until they appear eternal. At other times it is the inviting roses, reds, ambers, purples and golds of a sunset that make the sky a heaven and throw a path out over the water that runs to your feet and beckons you to step onto it. When the sun is not there the heaping up of clouds, shape upon shape, grey upon grey, play out large patterns of light and shade as though some painterly genius had swirled a mighty brush with powerful strokes. The shades of green that blanket the trees under this sky are exhilarating to comprehend. The deep tones that hang beneath the trees and wander their shadows like children playing hide and seek, the bright emeralds, the mosses, the yellow-greens and the silvered greens, the blue-greens – they are all pleasing to the eye and restful for the mind.

Late, late at night perhaps it is loveliest – on a still night when the air is bracing and your breath mists in front of you. The sky hangs emptied of clouds and filled with stars, stars which glow out their fineness as if attempting to communicate with your soul by their glistenings. I have wondered what their code is so as to decipher their language.

But the language of the land I know. It permeates my blood and the bond created can never be broken. The rhythm of the land will be part of my pulse forever. Its influence cannot be taken away – it is too late for that. There is a unique beauty to the rhythm of our land, a charm, a warmth, a certain happiness. But there is also a downbeat. It stings the ears and rattles mercilessly like a lambeg drum. The strains of all that I love have so far overcome this deeper tone but the tune which it plays cannot be ignored. It often drowns out the tune which I love and I must search like many others to find it again. It is the constant fury of political turmoil and religious controversy.

At a personal level it becomes the pressure of being the child of a man who leads in both these areas of public life. To form words to describe the emotions – private and tender – which are touched upon, is difficult. Words are inadequate when separated from physical contact with the hearer. This aspect of my relationship with Dad is unavoidable, so it is important to deal with its implications. The deepest of my feelings, though, shall, remain mine alone. There is always something about themselves which a person cannot and will not express.

My father is a quiet and considerate man. When I walk into his study in the early hours of a morning (for it is only then that he has time to study) to kiss him goodnight or ask for a little of his time to discuss a problem or obtain advice, I think as I see him, 'I really love you, Dad' and whatever it is that I am coming to him about shrinks into insignificance when I think of the mass of work he does. At times I just say goodnight and do not bother him with what is on my mind. Not that it would be a bother, for he has yet to turn me away, but I just do not have the heart to weigh in with something else!

At times I hate that factor in my father's life. Everything he does is of such vital importance that its wrong outcome would be disastrous. He is dealing with matters of church and state. If he makes a wrong move he would not be the only loser. If one of his children were to 'let the side down' it would be him who would be made to feel it most, and all that he has stood for and achieved would have sour taste. It would not be ruined I am sure, but it would be tainted. It would be like biting on a silver filling. I suppose, in its most naked form, this is responsibility. To whom much is given, much is required – I cannot dispute that I have been given much.

Dad does not reserve his sensitive and caring nature just for his family. He is concerned about the small matters of political and church responsibility as well as the main issues and has sense enough not to delegate these to the extent of self-elimination. The pressures upon his time are unbelievable. He has the ability to cope with a heavy schedule; in fact his is a constitution which thrives on work. He is not a workaholic. He enjoys relaxation as much as his work but he has, as Cherith and I tease him, 'a (Free) Presbyterian work ethic'. If he walks in and we are sitting reading he declares:

'It's well for you girls, sitting there reading, and your Da' an 'oul man of 60 working to this hour of the night'. The point is that it was he who taught us to love reading, and if we had been glued to the 'box' he would have scolded us for not reading!

Being in the position of leadership which he is, he cannot afford to lose touch with grass-roots opinion. Yet delegation is vital for any leader, nobody can do everything and the development of those around you is an important part of leadership. Those who work with Dad, both in church and party in the role of assistants are faithful to him in their representation. It is no easy position for anyone to serve. Many times they are accused of being 'yes men' to Dad, and we as a family know these colleagues are far from that! They are honest and forthright in their relationship and tell the truth whether it is favourable or not. My father is no wimp who needs his ego buffered by 'yes men'. These colleagues are loyal men and not only is their work appreciated by us, but their true friendship is a precious commodity. This friendship spans our family. I trust they feel and know how greatly we appreciate them. It is important in life to show thankfulness.

While Dad is a strong and determined man, he is not hard nor cold in his dealings with people or with us. I have watched younger men enter politics – I was no more than twelve or thirteen years of age when they began their careers – and in their development they have cut a cold sculpture – very white and still. I can understand their being so because political life is a difficult and often discouraging life in this province, yet I cannot help but wonder why they choose to portray an image of stoicism when all the while it is at their hand to display warmth. This is part of the downbeat of Ulster which is difficult to appreciate.

Sculpture of the hardest marble can still be enlivened by the artist's power to radiate the warmth of flesh itself. But I do not like this form of distance between a politician and his people and shall be eternally grateful that my father is not of this genre. His influence on the Democratic Unionist Party in this respect must be one of the greatest contributions a leader can make. It instills into its structure the importance not of principles, not of power but of people. Should his successor omit to be a vehicle of this manly humanity he will lose the essence of what the DUP came into being for.

I believe Dad's ministry reflects this same theme. Simultaneously in Ulster, my father has lived to see the establishment of both his denomination and his political party. He has not departed in either of these from the motives which originated them. There is more pressure upon him now than we as a family have ever witnessed, and my heart is often sorry for the sharp, ready criticism levelled at him and his work. When it comes from men who are where they are today because of his leadership, it is particularly rancid. I think it falls hard upon a man who is not self-seeking, when, for such tiny gain, fierce words of condemnation and accusation are used. That is part

of the downbeat which jars upon the hearing and strikes such
a deep note of sourness; it maims the kind melody and dispels
so abruptly its charm.

It is a lesson not easily forgotten to watch Dad refuse to
allow these things to become grudges. He lets the opponent
go his own way. He fights his corner at the time, I know that
well! But when the match is played he accepts the result. He
considers it as much a sin to be offended as to offend. His
strength lies in the fact that he can put the incident behind him
and move on. Surely this is what keeps him gentle and it is an
aspect of my father which I seek most to emulate. How many
hours are wasted by people moping over a past event, pessi-
mistic about its outcome, rehashing it over and over again until
the only reason they move is because there is so much débris
they have to! Their direction is dictated by that débris which
is usually piled up in front of them, so they have to move
backwards!

Dad is of course viewed by many as the composer of the
tune – the flagbearer for Ulster in this present situation. Along
with this comes an interest in the private life of the man and
in that of his family. This attitude is no new phenomenon for
those in public life. Nor is it likely to change. Nonetheless for
those concerned it is a very real hurdle which has to be taken.
To run to the rhythm is not easy. Keeping the pace I find is
becoming more difficult as I grow older. 'Doing what is right'
ironically takes on a different meaning. No offspring wants to
permit themselves to slide into what is perceived as their
father's mould just because it is convenient for a portion of
society.

The conflict arises because there is a certain loyalty between
the child and the parent which is hesitant to permit itself to be
misused. I have learnt to hold my tongue when often words
want to explode into the conversation, simply because my
sentiments would not be understood. They are weighed along
with my background, my name, my father's beliefs and the
Ten Commandments! In other words they are not taken on
their own merits. Can you imagine if you went into a super-
market and the checkout assistant threw all your items onto a

scale and guessed their cost – after taking the items of everyone else one at a time? It surely would be an unfair assessment. There would be the odd occasions when it would work to your advantage, but for the most it would not . . .

It is not easy to accept that private matters and views will be thrown into public light. Having a father who understands his children's needs, to feel and find freedom of self-expression, evidences to them the confidence he has in his role as their father – and in his own beliefs. Mum and Dad encouraged us in whatever particular area of interest we had. This has been our greatest safeguard. It presents a route to or a means of finding seclusion; a privacy, a retreat if you like, which is able to shield our individuality. For me it is art, and that is a pleasant rhythm to trace. I suppose the glare of publicity upon Dad has made each of us very aware of the importance of respect for the other's privacy.

It is the compound effect of this aspect of life which creates interest from others. Dad has always been 'known' as far as we are concerned. His appearance in the headlines did not come overnight. We grew up with it. So, people now ask things like 'What is it like being Ian Paisley's daughter?' Where in the world do you begin? There is no point of comparison – I never knew anything else.

A question which has been asked in almost every interview I have undertaken is; 'What would your father do if you brought home a Roman Catholic boyfriend?' I honestly reckon it would be a lot harder for the poor guy to explain it to his family than for me to mine! What do the interviewers want to hear? That Dad would turf me out into the street? I know for a fact that he would not. The hospitality he would show would be the same as to any Protestant boyfriend. His concern would be from the point of view of dating someone unsaved, and their particular religious tendencies would be secondary. As I claim Christ as my Saviour I know that Dad expects my dating relationships to be in line with that.

As a matter of fact I did once have a crush on a guy who turned out to be a Roman Catholic. I was no more than fourteen at the time. He had very nice blue eyes, I remember – and they were not too close together! I met him while swimming. He was with a few friends and I was with my older sister. Sharon was never without a boyfriend and usually, well to be honest, always was much more sensible in her behaviour. We were on holidays at the time. Sharon couldn't swim so she kept to the shallow end of the pool. The guys were carrying on a bit and we all got involved in a game of water polo. This went on for two or three days – not continuously, of course. One evening, the swimmer with the nice eyes suggested afterwards that we go for a walk around the grounds of the place we were staying, which were extensive and very pleasant. His friend was going to come with Sharon who wasn't too interested because she had a boyfriend at home. Anyway, we let Mum and Dad know we were all going for a walk and were told to be back at the hotel by 10 o'clock. Somehow we got separated from Sharon and the other boy, and as our walk was going quite well, neither of us drew attention to that fact. It slipped our attention also that it was after the 10 o'clock deadline! Naturally, my father took a stroll to make sure that everything was OK. We were, by this time, on our way back to the hotel (honestly!) and having come alongside the tennis courts and not too far from the hotel entrance, I was being given a 'goodnight kiss' when Dad happened to round the corner.

'Rhonda, what are you doing?' (Not that it wasn't obvious.) 'It's after 10 o'clock. You'd better come in.' I've never known a kiss to end so abruptly! As we all walked back towards the hotel, Dad talked very casually. He wasn't cross. I think he was more surprised. After all, I was too! I'd never been kissing anyone before when Dad was around.

'What's your name, young man?'

'Dermot.' (Dermot is almost invariably a Roman Catholic name.)

'Flippin' heck,' I thought. 'Why couldn't he have said William or something?' Dad looked at me, rolled his eyes and grinned in disbelief.

'Cheerio!' we all said as we reached the hotel entrance. Dad and I crossed the porchway, and stopped at the bottom of the ornate stairway.

'That's ridiculous, Rhonda. Don't you behave like that again. Get away upstairs to your bed, you silly wee girl.' He bent over and kissed me goodnight on the head and smiled down at me. 'Whew!' I thought as I headed upstairs. I did see the boy several times after that in the swimming pool and we always had a good laugh. He never did suggest another walk but every so often when I missed the ball during the games we played, he'd say to me in a vaguely familiar voice, 'Rhonda, what are you doing?' The incident was never mentioned again. We had a perfect understanding over the matter. Dad had absolutely nothing against our association in the swimming pool, but the limitation had been set and I wasn't about to question it. Dad didn't get stuck into a mighty lecture that night because there was no need. I knew that he had enough authority to forbid me to see the guy again. He chose not to use his authority in that way because it was not necessary in this case. I have always respected him for knowing when and how to exercise his parental authority over us. Because my father does not provoke his children to wrath, our task of obeying him is made easy.

It never ceases to amaze me how many people want to believe that he is a harsh father. It would be an impossibility for me to try and assess how Dad must feel when he sees pressure being put on his children. Firstly, as a female, my response is bound to differ. Secondly, I have no experience of parenthood and cannot, therefore, measure that protective spirit which I imagine is inherent in parenthood. But I know that there is a fine line between caring and interfering. One thing which my parents have never done is interfere. Dad expects us to make our own decisions. He will help and advise but he will not push us one way or another. He is often accused of it, and I usually get the remark,

'Sure, you had no choice in the matter, yer Da' wouldn't have let you!' or,

'Your father has you well versed for this one!' as if Dad calls us in each day and goes over what he expects of us. Generally, we all can laugh this off but sometimes we hear it once too often in the middle of a rough week when work is piled high, and when there is an abundance of things needing attention and not enough hours in the day to accomplish all that must be done. Then it becomes a beat that cannot be matched The pace is too demanding and its effects are as strong on private matters and relationships as on public and work related matters.

One December a youth died. He was a Roman Catholic and I had been involved with his situation through the youth work which I do. His death was a tragic accident as the result of drug abuse. I knew him for about three years and saw him on a weekly basis, sometimes twice a week. He was a punk. I called for his girlfriend on the morning of the funeral and took her, along with some other friends of his, to the chapel where the service was to take place. It was a cold, drizzly morning and everything appeared monochrome. Even the splendour of punk colour was absent. I had met with the boy's parents at the hospital during the days he had lain unconscious and I had visited their home since. They were a very nice family and had a lovely home. As I drew my car into the side of the road, the funeral procession came along. It passed the side of the car and the punks began to get out to join it. It was very strange. My instinct was also to go into the building to join with the mourners yet no-one expected it. I was a Protestant – not just nominally, but by faith. To attend a service which would proclaim that this youth could still be prayed and paid into heaven and a sacrifice offered by a priest for his sins, contradicted all that I believed about salvation free from works, confessionals and penance. Yet had I not been Rhonda *Paisley*, I am quite sure that at that moment, when moved by the loss of a person whom I cared for, I would have attended the service and sat with the punks. As it was, I had to accept the unspoken understanding between the other mourners and me. They all moved into the chapel grounds, not expecting me to come. I watched them go in through the doors and stood alone by the roadside, wondering why it mattered. The rhythm of Ulster at such times is beyond my comprehension. Not many months before, I had attended a funeral service in a Protestant church. I had heard nothing from the minister that day about salvation, I had heard no proclamation given to the mourners of Calvary's atonement, yet nobody would care whether Rhonda Paisley was in attendance or not. I knew once again the rhythm of the land in all its frustration and hypocrisy, and my mourning was left to itself. That evening, Dad asked me how things had gone. 'Did you go into the service?' 'No, Dad. I didn't.' He just nodded and gave me a hug. It is this mutual understanding which my father has taken time to establish and maintain between each of us as his children which cheers my soul when I feel constrained to action of which I am unsure and uncomfortable about.

Building a relationship within the bounds of unwanted yet imposed restrictions is a delicate business. To be honest I never really noticed that aspect of things until I was faced directly with it during my first year at university. I was not dating any one person very steadily. I had a few good friends and some I saw more than others. Among them, one in particular was really good fun to be with and we began to see a bit more of each other. After a few weeks we had our first serious conversation and our last! It seemed to come out of the blue. He brought the subject up by saying that he had been thinking about my Dad quite a lot recently, and the work which he did, and we talked about politics in Ulster and the situation there. He was American and his knowledge of the history and the background of our troubles was minimal and very pro-Republican. He had many questions which I tried to answer fairly, explaining to the best of my ability the differences of opinion which existed. Eventually the course of the conversation altered. The next time we could see each other was exactly one week later because we were both working and our schedules did not coincide until then. We met for lunch and he was as good company as ever. As we walked to a lecture afterwards, he said,

'Rhonda, I've decided not to date you anymore.' I just looked at him – waiting for the punch-line of what was obviously a joke! 'I'm being serious here,' he said and I realised that he was. 'I've really been thinking about Ireland and your family and your Dad and I just don't think I can handle that. I don't want to be involved in all it would mean.' I don't know what he expected me to say. Frankly, I couldn't quite believe what I heard and so just smiled and said,

'Fine.'

'Fine?' he repeated.

'Yes,' I said with a laugh. 'Fine. It's your choice. I can't make you date me and if that's your reason, that's your reason.'

'You mean you aren't mad?' he asked.

'Do I look it?' I asked. We both laughed. I headed on through the lecture room doors and they swung closed. I only ever saw him around the campus and in an occasional lecture. We always shouted hello to one another, and I often have thought it would be nice to be able to walk away from a name like that!

It is not what we as a family set ourselves up to be, but it is the concept which people build that it is impossible to be immune from. The most serious aspect of this takes the love which exists between us and plays on its loyalties as a means of obtaining what is wanted or expected. I was visited one afternoon by a man who obviously held quite different opinions from me on several things. For him these were very important matters which he felt reflected one's spiritual condition. He let me know these opinions and why he felt that my not adhering to them was detrimental to my father! The list was fairly extensive. His whole focus was on the fact that I was hurting my father's testimony and that for his sake I ought to alter these things. I felt that my relationship with Dad was the bargaining point, that I had to prove my love by doing certain things. How shallow would the love be, I thought, if it depended on tokens in which I did not believe! I must admit I was amazed that day at the extent to which people wish to have control over the behaviour of the family of men in leadership. It upset me, but funnily enough, it didn't anger me, that others preferred an appearance, a look, a certain set of guidelines that caused them no problems with the people they knew and the things they did. I am glad my father tuned our ears to the melodies of the land that have a depth and a lasting song. Those which match the heart, the inner being, not just the outward form. I think, in fact, I am sure that no matter where I go, this is the music of the land which I can never lose.

Top: From left to right: Sharon, Mum with Cherith, and Rhonda.
Bottom: Cherith, Mum, Sharon, Dad and Rhonda.

1987: Mum and Dad celebrate another election victory.

Top: 1988: Family photograph. Back: Dad and Mum. Front from left: Kyle, Cherith, Rhonda, Ian. **Bottom:** The early days of Dad's political career.

Dad and I walking Bishop in the early morning.

It is hard to accept on a very soft night as you walk through a park or a forest, or on a quiet afternoon as you kick the sand on a beach, or on an early winter morning when dark, skinny silhouettes of leafless trees reach through the dewy mist, that this place, this land which at that moment is so still, is so broken with the conflict of the past twenty years. I have learnt to leave many things to themselves and to let people think and say what they like, for the rhythm of Ulster has a sense of cynicism that is capable of warping and distorting.

Ulster people I love, they are my fellow citizens. I hope their loyalties will not deceive them into thinking that the downbeat of the land is the true orchestration of the soul. It is all too easy to become a victim of your own rhetoric and propaganda.

To be a true loyalist, or even a unionist, 'The Sash' doesn't have to be your favourite tune, and to be redeemed and fundamentalist in your faith does not mean that you can't enjoy a good party nor wear a pair of earrings! Such little peeves may help as far as favour with some goes, but, thank God, they are not prerequisites for heaven!

I try to concentrate on what has been set before me to do. When the downbeat becomes too loud, I have, until now, always found the love of the softer rhythm and in my sense of failure, I find again the means of success through its creator. I have a fear that this may not always be so. Often, incidents have caused us as a family to refer to the fact that because of Dad's position there are certain things that follow. I thank him for teaching me by example that 'the land is the Lord's' and for never expecting nor demanding that his children keep pace to a beat that is not of their choosing.

CHAPTER SIX

'Vote Paisley'

'Paisley is our leader, we shall not be moved. Paisley is our leader, we shall not be moved . . .' The familiar tune sang its proclamation once again along the victory parade route in the streets of Ballymena. I hated the tune and I hated the words yet I joined in their declaration with as much joy as the others, running alongside the landrover that carried Mum, Dad and Uncle Jim, Dad's Election Agent. The band's beat, the enthusiasm of the people waving from windows and doors, the growing numbers who walked behind as the parade wove its way round the town. How could you not allow yourself to be swept up onto its plane of happiness? It would be sacrilege to miss the delight and I never have yet, no matter how long and uphill Dad's election trails have been.

'Vote Paisley' was first used regarding my mother. As a child, I remember running into Mum and Dad's bedroom, clad in fluffy pink PJs at the scratch of dawn, with my older sister by my side to ask, 'Did you win this time, Mummy?' Mum and Dad were obviously exhausted because at that time in Ulster the count was immediately after close of polls – now it is held back until the next day. 'Yes, dear, we won,' replied Mum with a sleepy smile. 'You will have to call her Councillor now, girls,' said Dad joking, as he drew Mum to himself. 'Now get back to bed for a while.' But Sharon and I were too excited to sleep again and speculated on all that being a councillor might mean. 'Paisley tops the poll,' was one paper's headline, and for the life of me I couldn't figure out its meaning until Sharon imparted to me the fact that 'poll' was quite different from 'pole'! I have a vivid recollection of two visits to the City Hall when I was a child. One took place in the car park. Mum, Sharon, and I were there and the then Lord Mayor, Geddis, was crossing the courtyard. Mum pointed him out and explained who he was. To our young eyes he was ancient and as he had a rather crinkled visage, we instantly named him 'Geddis the Lettuce' and from that day to this, I'm afraid the position of Lord Mayor has never struck me with any awe whatsoever! It's strange, I suppose, but because my father cuts a very strong figure by his standing alone, wee men – by wee I mean notably small in height – tend to amuse me greatly when I see them in positions of authority. All this power and aura of position – then they stand up and I'm in fits! There was once an Alliance leader in Ulster who came across as very haughty. He had only been known to me by way of television until one day I was going to Stormont with Dad to hear a debate and he came waddling across the huge, ornate hall, his little bum wiggling behind – not that it could have wiggled anywhere else! Instantly my mind sang, 'How much is that doggy in the window? – the one with the waggly tail?' I will never forget how shocked I was to see all the height of it, and funnily enough, from that day to this, the Alliance Party has always been a farce to me!

The second recollection of the City Hall was when Mum had Sharon and me with her on another occasion. It was still possible to take members of the family into the Members' Room at the time. Now, due to its abuse by Republicans, this has been altered and only Members of Council can use it. Gerry Fitt of the Catholic SDLP was a Member of Council then, and he was standing at one of the tables reading the paper. Mum introduced us to him. He, of course, called Mum 'Eileen' and as a child, I thought him really cheeky to do so, seeing that he and Dad were always against each other. What a perspective a child's mind has! I do not hold any more respect for Gerry Fitt now than I did as a youngster. I would find it most difficult to take the attitude that some would seem to evidence that as a member of the House of Lords he has 'seen the light'. A more accurate description would be that 'he has as many faces as the Albert Clock'. I don't think one can take a British Lordship and expect it to erase the damage caused by previous activities.

Apart from being aware of press attention around Mum and anything she said, Council never really meant a great deal of difference to our lives. My mother was determined that it would not rob us of time with her, not would she see our needs overlooked because of her political involvement. Even when later she sat in Stormont for both Assembly and Convention, we never lost attention, care and understanding from her. If she could not get home, she always 'phoned and we were never placed in a position of anxiety as to what might have happened. My mother is an immensely kind woman. She is a lady – never pushy or arrogant, never vain or obnoxious. She has strong views and an intelligent wit. Her humour can cut like a knife, and so can her tongue if need be, but all that she does is touched by her gracious spirit and her loving nature. How often while doing my own council work, I have heard constituents say, 'When your mother represented us she did this or that . . .' Take it from me – it's a high standard to have to live up to.

The slogan 'Vote Paisley' has applied more often, of course, to Dad. Elections are second nature to Ulster and to our household. Dad campaigns like a trooper. He covers every inch of his constituency at a rare speed and nothing deters him. He never believes that he is going to win – he works as though each election is his first. Then, when polls close, he says, 'Well, we've done our best.' It is a good theory: nobody ought to take anyone's vote for granted.

I believe voting ought to be compulsory and if there is no candidate you support, you can always destroy your paper. But at least everyone would be fulfilling their responsibility and not abdicating when it comes to electing a Government. There have been times when an adverse attitude towards voting has made me angry. Several instances come to mind. I will use one as an example.

A wealthy man had many business concerns and was in difficulty. He immediately came to my father as his M.P. and Dad managed to get the case solved in his favour, saving him thousands of pounds. As he, due to his religious views, did not vote, he refused to admit that he had come to Dad to get the case handled. 'I got it all sorted out myself,' he retorted to a friend of ours who had initially suggested he go to Dad. The friend knew he had seen Dad simply because he had told him that he would possibly be hearing from him and Dad, of course, said, 'I already have.' Dad just laughed when he heard and said,

'Typical!'

I said, 'Flippin' Pharisee!' and Dad said,

'Now, Rhonda!' looking up over his glasses with a grin. It will be a grand day when such Pharisees vote in Ulster by law.

After the count all I ever want to do is hibernate for a week. That is an impossibility because the weeks of campaigning mean that work gets behind and the first priority has to be to clear the backlog.

Despite the hours and the politics, though, electioneering always turns out to have amusing times to remember. These seem to become more hilarious as the years go on. During an election week (we were all youngsters at the time), Mum had the five of us out in the car. Ian was amusing us by pulling faces and mimicking people. A woman passer-by stopped and gazed into the car and saw cause for offence. She opened the door and gave a mouthful to my brother. We were all frozen in shock at this unexpected outburst. She shut the door and we all began to roar with laughter.

'She's got the cheek – interfering old bag – look at her! You should have told her! What would she know, with bony knees like that?' I just had the words out and we were laughing the harder now – when Ian rolled the window down and shouted over to her,

'What would you know? Sure, you've got bony knees!' Again we were in shock, this time at Ian. The woman was really mad now and came over, hardly able to walk because of her efforts to hoist her skirt up above her knees.

'Bony knees! I haven't bony knees – look!' she squealed, placing her varicose-veined, thick, 30 denier stockinged leg on the door. The five of us could no longer be held responsible to behave in a mannerly way and laughter reigned supreme. Mum had just begun her approach to the car as the woman was leaving.

'What was all that about?' she asked. We related the story.

'You didn't say that to her, surely Ian?'

'Rhonda told me to,' was his excuse.

'Ah well, we'll not lose her vote anyway, seeing this is Belfast and Dad is in North Antrim,' was my excuse.

It is rare that elections ever occur here during good weather. Usually it rains and more print ends up on jacket sleeves than through letter boxes! The General Election in 1987 must have been the wettest yet. Every day a little troop of us headed to Ballymena to Uncle Jim and Auntie Margaret's house. There we got our instructions and were well equipped with stickers, news sheets and any other hand-out in vogue that day. The speakers were mounted on the car and suitable decorations were added, and we were off. Ian, Cherith and I always stayed with each other and we worked in turns driving, speaking over the loud-hailer and forking out the literature. It was Ian's turn to shove the news sheets through the doors. I was driving and Cherith was speaking. Cherith decided to break from the little Party/Paisley repertoire we were using and began her next sentence.

'Come to your doors now and meet the one and only Ian Paisley, Junior, possibly your next M.P.! He's in the area now – don't miss this opportunity to shake his hand and speak to him about your concerns for the future!' Poor Ian stood in unbelief, his ego wilting before our eyes, an armful of soggy literature and his cap dripping rain down onto his nose. Doors opened, old women peeped through curtains, youngsters started to ask,

'Mister, are you really Paisley's son?' Up and down the street we went, everyone now enjoying the spirit – even Ian, who has never had to drink as many cups of tea in his life. Our conclusion? It's one sure way of arousing interest from voters on a miserable rainy afternoon.

The 1987 General Election came and went. To my recollection though, it was the most difficult to muster enthusiasm for. We have so many elections in Ulster and none alter the speed of change here. We go and vote. We hold our feelings and abide by the law. We still have terrorism and we still have an absentee government in control. Local government has been rendered inadequate in Northern Ireland by the present Act in existence. Westminster chooses to ignore the wishes of the majority and the voices of our M.P.s are treated with contempt by English politicians who are too insufferably arrogant to listen. Is it any wonder that this upcoming generation in Ulster is rethinking their forefathers' thoughts and learning that the Union is only meaningful if and when its principles are intact.

The term 'Vote Paisley' has in turn been applied to me although if my campaign merits had been solely responsible for my election I'd never have become a councillor in 1985. For most of the time, the campaigning was enjoyable and busy, but it had its moments. I was shoving a handbill through a letter-box – it was one of those boxes that are lined inside with a brush draught excluder – and to get a flimsy bill through I folded it. As it penetrated the brush it flipped open just in time to send a dainty little ornament whizzing up the hallway. Along another road was a home for the blind. I knocked on the door; a lady answered. With my reason for calling explained, I asked if I could come in and speak to the residents.

'Certainly dear, but it would be better if you could come back after lunch. This morning they have a seminar on.'

'O.K. That will be fine,' I replied. 'May I leave this literature for them to have a look at?' She looked at me as though I'd sprung horns.

'They're blind, dear.' Oops! I thought – there goes another dozen votes. Somehow, enough votes were cast to give me the privilege of serving as a councillor in the Laganbank Area of South Belfast, and when polls closed that day, I for one, was glad to remove the 'Vote Paisley' posters we had pasted and hung all over the area!

Political involvement contrasts more with my outlook as an artist than does anything else. Art knows no boundary when it comes to turning an idea into the reality of a work. The idea comes, inspired by some movement of light over an object or by the awakening of some sense to the pleasantness of an instant. To transform the idea into a state of existence, I paint until the idea goes because it is replaced by the actual result. In executing the physical painting, every sense is used and played upon and any medium is legitimate. In politics, senses have to be bridled. The ideal has to be conformed to the bounds of law and tradition. Conformity and compromise are essentials for political survival whereas the same are destructive for the artist. Should conformity be the artist's aim, his imagination is instantly stifled. Should compromise of his view rule his outlook, he is fettered and the uniqueness that could be imparted is lost. I believe the most inspirational aspect of life is the ordinary and in that alone politics blends with my art to deepen, I hope, its comprehension of life and beautify the mundane, but this is the only pleasing aspect of politics that I have encountered.

Perhaps the most pathetic side of politics to watch is in those who have found much that is attractive in position alone and for whom clinging to a position is their sheer motivation in life. How they wangle to get a chairmanship! And any committee in existence – they somehow manage to get on to it. Why, I constantly wonder, do they want it? I feel duty bound to let them have their wee desire for truly they are so pitiful, but I thank God in the same instant that there is more to life than committees. In one of our Stormont offices I read a pretty creased up poster: 'God so loved the world that He didn't send a committee.' I laughed in agreement as I read it and, asking why it was a little worse for wear, was told that it had been thrown into the waste bin a few times – by Dad! – but had always managed to get rescued. So there it hung, a little worse for wear – but still readable and still true.

When events led to my own involvement in Council at least (because of my background) I was aware of some of the pitfalls. I was not expecting, however, to learn as much as I have regarding loyalty and honest speaking. When my father makes a political statement, it is very straight. He doesn't try to deceive his audience. If they don't like what he is saying – they don't like it. But he will say it just the same. Being used to the fact that what Dad speaks publicly is what he says privately, certainly had implanted in me the false belief that all those who agreed with Dad publicly did so privately as well. I wasn't too long into things when the light went on and I realised how dim my sight had been until then. One such rude awakening came at a businessmen's function. A then aspiring politician whom I have to admit, I had held in respect, was present and turned out to be using the function as a platform for his own promotion. He, in cunning form, was well declaring his case – but what a totally different one it was to his media presentation and his public style. Yet it was smoothly worded so that he could escape if any accusation was levelled. I felt my immaturity. I saw the complications in such a harsh light. I went home and rethought the evening's conversations and felt my being there suited one purpose only: that the Leader's daughter's presence indicated that the Leader knew.

Initially, I wondered why I had been invited. I had learned precisely why! It was not a pleasant lesson but I remain thankful for it and I am glad that I learnt it when I did. The course of that particular politician's career has been the more interesting to watch. It has altered considerably even from his own plan, I think. You can never serve two diverse aspirations pleading loyalty equally to them. Sooner or later a choice has to be made and by that stage it is impossible not to lose respect. Respect in Ulster politics is not easy to come by – once lost it simply isn't replaced. Until that night I truly had thought my political views were similar to this particular politician's. I experienced what I had often seen and heard others talk of in politics and the sour taste leaves a bitter trace. It does, however, potently remind us that confidence is misplaced if it is rested upon man's ability. I do not dislike the man, but I do no longer trust him, and I imagine that that doubt will colour every statement he makes. Perhaps to admit such feeling reflects most the changes that have occurred in me as a result of my own involvement in politics. There is a degree of cynicism which entwines itself now in my political outlook and there is also a deeper appreciation within for my father's honesty as a politician. He is a trustworthy politician: I have come across very few others.

There is a hardening aspect of political involvement also. You have to grit your teeth and ignore many voices of dissent. You have to take the irrational judgement of others, deliberately ignore its hurtfulness and keep on with the job. Personal sensitivities have to be set in a back seat position, otherwise politics are not universal but introverted.

I wonder often if Ulster has succeeded in removing from our natures piece by piece the ability to show outwardly our sorrow within. The sad agony traces its print and every death engraves again the terrible finality of life taken, but outwardly our expression of grief is one of stoicism – the old 'stiff upper lip'. How, after so many years of destruction, can sympathy be expressed any more in meaningful terms? At such times failure to change the hot vapour of anger and care into form depicts only feminine failure. Every womanly instinct is cruelly distorted and left dulled, a mockery of its creator's intention. I imagine that a man feels the same incapacity of his manliness to become a legitimate force of healing and repair. There is a dilemma for the child of God in Ulster politics. It is not an excuse to shy away from being active, but it does mean it is often necessary to forsake popularity in order to do whatever can be done to repair what has been broken. It is a delusion to think that the child of God ought only to be involved in the niceties of bridge building, when in fact they ought to be involved in the mucky side also. It means rolling up your sleeves, it means getting dirty, it means sweat and tiredness, and it means disapproval from others.

The greatest dilemma that I have found on a daily basis in politics is the presence of IRA Sinn Fein in Council. These, whom the British Government have permitted to hold office in Ulster, yet with whom they say they won't meet, openly declare allegiance to terrorism as a legitimate way of obtaining what they aim for politically. Our Party policy is to prevent them from being heard and it is to ostracize them socially. I cannot pretend that it is not difficult to walk into a room that has IRA Sinn Fein members present and speak to everyone but them. It is not a natural thing to meet someone in a corridor and not nod a 'hello'. But all this must be placed on the larger scale, and it is, I believe, more hypocritical to express social graces to gunmen than to treat them with the contempt they deserve. I'm afraid you have to stand imaginatively where the widow or orphan stands in order to keep yourself from falling prey to Northern Ireland Office propaganda. The price of my freedom has been too highly paid for to have petty social graces wean me from the cause hundreds have given their lives in.

There is a portion in the Book of Isaiah that I find optimistic and very helpful when such considerations must be made, and difficult decisions backed by action. It is Chapter 43 and includes these words:

> Fear not, for I have redeemed thee, I have called thee by thy name; thou art mine. When thou passest through the waters, I will be with thee; and through the rivers, they shall not overflow thee; when thou walkest through the fire, thou shall not be burned: neither shall the flame kindle upon thee . . . since thou wast precious in my sight, thou hast been honourable, and I have loved thee . . . fear not, for I am with thee.

I do not know of any greater comfort than simply remembering I am redeemed, nor is there any thought that so powerfully subdues my rebellious spirit than this. Its responsibility puts sanity into my life, yet it permits my joy to laugh out its happiness and it takes me as I am and loves me. I am baffled when very strict, hyper-Fundamentalist Christians tell me art and art-oriented matters are devilish, unspiritual pursuits, yet they are up to their ears in politics! I doubt that there is anything more corrupting than politics.

God only knows how many more times 'Vote Paisley' will be applicable in elections in Ulster, and I daresay even Dad's enemies would agree that an election in Ulster without Paisley in the running would be a quieter and less exciting campaign!

Dad wouldn't honestly be too worried – in fact, like all of us in his family, he would find it a happy relief.

'Vote Paisley.' Many have – and he's yet to let them down!

CHAPTER SEVEN

Holy Days and Holidays

Sunday for many people that I know is a peaceful, quiet and very routine day of their week. A nice lie-in, breakfast in bed, morning worship, family lunch, a good sleep, evening service, supper and an early night. That Sunday could be one sweep of activity from the minute your feet hit the floor until they drag you back up the stairs to bed at night is incomprehensible. Sundays are always like that for us! I'm afraid that no matter how well organized we are, there is always something to shatter the calm and the old devil always gets the blame. The car keys get lost, the dog gets out, the hairdryer breaks, a list of announcements goes astray, the gate jams (yet again). You name it – we get it on a Sunday. I have yet to meet a minister's family who didn't know what I am talking about. And when eventually we all arrive and are seated here and there throughout the congregation, and when Dad walks up the pulpit steps in his spotless black frock coat and sharp white clerical collar, it's hard to believe that minutes before, there was a full alert!

It tickles me when people say things to us like, 'Oh, I don't know how you do it, you are all so organized,' or, 'Your family are never ruffled, are they?' If only they knew! The fact is that such statement makers are the type who wouldn't believe you if you were to offer graphic details of the pandemonium. The Paisley family, to them, are irreproachable, and while I do sincerely appreciate their form of affection and loyalty, I could

nonetheless wring their necks at times. How often I have got
mouth ulcers as a result of biting my lip in the midst of a
spell of such idolatry is beyond count. I am reminded of my
hypocrisy for the rest of the week every time I eat something
salty and console myself with the proverb which says even a
fool when he holdeth his tongue is considered wise. I wonder
if biting your lip is on a par!

Church-going, of course, has always been an important
aspect of the week for the family. The sanctity of the Sabbath
is a way of life. As a youngster, Dad learned to find pleasure
in this day of worship and that element of a Sunday has been
fused into our home life also. This pigment is missing in many
homes when it comes to a Sunday. The majority of my friends
when I was a child hated Sunday. It was long and boring and
for those who knew their parents held no convictions about
Sunday – it was a blast!

Recently a friend and I were out with a man and his wife
who have over the years built a happy home and a strong,
prosperous business. Now, with their children adults and
happily married, they can relax a little and enjoy the fruit of
their work. They are kind and generous people. It was a
Monday when we were with them and it had become quite
late. My tiredness must have been apparent. The man
commented that he had better not keep us any longer for he
could see I was looking sleepy. One thing he went on to say
was that he wasn't usually tired on a Monday because he slept
most of Sunday. He hadn't been a church-goer since he had
left home as a young man. Church for him was 'downright
rotten'. He had been made to attend church four times on a
Sunday and it was 'a b . . . bore'. The result was he never
insisted on sending his kids anywhere. It was up to them what
they did when they were old enough 'and they've turned out
well just the same'. Who can blame him? I am quite sure I
would react in exactly the same way. Here was a perfect
example of the boring Sunday, dead preaching, rules and regu-
lations, straitjacketed kids – the whole purpose of Sunday
missed, the joy of worship replaced with the legal echo of a
commandment to remember the sabbath day. A cold shadowy

grey echo – not one of colour that reverberates and sings out its highlights. An echo with no tint of lustre and flat in its tone. This is a danger every child of God faces with the question of worship, that it becomes nothing more than a formality. There have been weeks, even months, when church-going has been practised by me only as an outward gesture. Inwardly, the desire to worship remains, and private communion with Christ no less frequent, but public worship has fallen simply into the category of duty. When this has been so I have always found it is because personal preparation for public worship has not been what it ought. Perhaps the reasons were legitimate but obviously they were out of correct sequence in my living and the corrective process does require time. Thankfully Christ is tender in his chastening and patient as he redirects. When church-going becomes a duty it is a mockery. It makes a sham of the privilege of honouring the King of Kings and it insults the fellow believers with whom the privilege is being shared. Most of all it hinders the working of the Holy Spirit in those present who are outside Christ. To raise children with a view of Sunday as a day of penance is to deprive them of what ought to be the most beneficial day of their week. The day which makes the following week-days of greater value. I cannot believe that the awesome picture on Mount Sinai is as strong in its impression on the soul and mind as that of the hand of concern that moved across the cold stone to engrave in warmth for mankind a set of laws to guide him in life.

I suppose having never known Sunday to be anything other than a day of activity, the temptation to become a literalist and make it 'a day of rest' will always be strong. I think for Dad this temptation is a good deal less potent than I find it to be. For him it is yet another time to proclaim Christ in the gospel ministry to which he has been called. That calling is the most important aspect of his life. Opportunity for service refuels him for the week's activity. The giving of himself poured out in his preaching acts as a means of sustenance for him spiritually. This appears almost a contradiction but often when there seems no more to give from within, a fresh impetus is secured and new stamina results, the kind of stamina which turns visions into realities, which makes the intransient, transient. In the cause of a Gospel ministry it is this dependence upon the power of a superior being, namely the Holy Spirit, which touches the lives of others so that life remade in Christ becomes a possibility for them also.

On holidays of course Sundays take on quite a different form. When we were youngsters all our holidays were spent in and around the United Kingdom – mainly Scotland and Wales.

One of the first things Dad always did was to go on the prowl for a 'decent' church which we could attend the coming Sunday. Now Dad's idea of a decent church is one preferably without a choir (which are only sources of problems, he says), one which uses only the King James Version of the Bible, and one which has no 'trappings of popery' about it. All this made the hunt quite exciting and certainly caused great anticipation in five kids as to whether or not there would be a choir to watch the faces of, an ecumenical clergyman, or the ultimate – whether or not we would walk out in protest! One thing for certain is that Dad's children all get involved in the spirit of the cause – the motives might at times be questionable, but the willingness is there!

At one such service away up in the Highlands of Scotland, all three of these possibilities merged to create an unforgettable morning worship. To begin with we had to drive for about forty-five minutes to get to this wee stone church. We were there five minutes early and our arrival doubled the congregation. There was a choir made up of two men and one very plain woman adorned in a cerise pink petalled hat (which could have done with a good watering). One of these men was the 'tuner' for the hymn-singing. Now this was something new to us – there was no organ or piano so he stood at the front, encaged in a highly polished wooden cubicle and went 'Hummm . . .' Then everybody began. It was more like a lament than the singing we were used to. This wee tuner amused us no end and even Dad's very long stares could not stifle our sniffles and giggles. The tuner's work was in vain anyway because Dad drowned everybody else out and he never sings in tune at the best of times! Sharon and I being the older two were supposed to be setting an example. Sharon had come up with a method of biting the end of her hanky which worked very well. Unfortunately I, as usual, had not brought a hanky and in no way would Sharon part with hers. Anyway we struggled through the Psalm singing which seemed to last as long as the 119th and the minister came forward to pray. He was in a two-tiered garment – black skirt and white smock. He was balding and wore glasses and had a rosy complexion which turned beautifully into deep scarlet as he recognised Dad.

The five of us watched in horror as he *read* his prayer and I think the ten amazed eyes which were upon him proved a bit off-putting. Next came the Scriptures and they weren't the KJV! One of my brothers leant over and in a huge whisper asked, 'Are we going to walk out, Daddy?' 'Shhhh!' Then came the exhortation. As this was beginning we noticed that the wee tuner had dozed off and his head was hanging in that precarious position which precedes a sudden twitch upright again. My other brother's attention had not been taken by this and upon hearing the sermon declared to Dad, 'That man's an apostate!' He was, and my father had had enough. He nodded to us, up we got and all trooped out, our little feet pattering noisily over the bare floorboards. Outside and into the car where we all at last could laugh without having to suck hankies. Even Dad could do nothing else but laugh. We headed off for what I contend was a well-earned lunch!

As time has passed we now aim to spend our holidays in countries where English is not the spoken language. That way we get Dad to ourselves. Selfish? Yes! But it does get a bit much when you walk into churches and the pastor gives Dad a special welcome and promptly calls on him to preach.

Besides this, you have to travel a fair distance to get away from Ireland's problems. When we were very young, and before Dad entered politics, we spent our summer holidays in a house which we rented in a tiny, out of the way place called Killowen. It was a small, one-storey whitewashed building with a bright blue half-door. The water supply was brought in from a spring well beside the house. It stood at the top of a little hill. At the base of the hill my paternal grandparents owned a house, alongside which ran a beautiful loose stone wall with a stile over it which in turn led to my aunt and uncle's property, and from there a path worn into existence by man's feet, continued on up to our house. For many years Killowen was where we spent our holidays. Our cousins on Mum's side of the family came in shifts to spend time with us and we had tremendous adventures in the hillside and shores and then at night by the heat of the open fire inside, we talked and ate.

It was another sort of fire which eventually ended our holidays there, though. My grandparents' house was burned down and the whole place daubed with IRA slogans. We could not return.

As time went on, any holiday near to home was likely to become an ongoing political seminar on the Irish Question. We learnt that lesson well another summer when due to work circumstances we remained in the province for the summer holiday season. By way of a change, we stayed in a house in Kilkeel for a couple of weeks. It would have been much more restful simply to have stayed in our own house – there was more space, and at least when constituency problems were being handled, all the necessary stationery, etc. was at hand. It honestly was like a twenty-four hour drop-in centre, and my father is the sort who turns nobody away. Right enough when you start and listen to their particular difficulties, it is impossible to tell a person to get lost, but I must admit we all did come very close to it on one or two occasions! During that holiday my brothers were carrying on and started chasing one another round the place. They were roaring with laughter over something, I don't know what, as they teased each other. In the front door, through one room, down the hall, across the kitchen, out the glass-panelled back door – Ian was flying after Kyle. Meanwhile someone came in through the back door and closed it. In the front door the boys raced, down the hall again, across the kitchen, Kyle still first, out through the back door – this time literally! A mighty crash followed, with a mightier yell. In one second everybody, police guards included, were at the spot. Kyle was sitting on the ground looking like a ghost bedecked in glitter and Ian was standing over him looking like an anaemic ghost! Kyle was responsible for the mighty crash and Ian for the yell of horror. No doubt the speed at which this feat had been performed proved his lifesaver, because the worst cut was on the palm of his hand; any other scratches were not even deep. We renamed the town 'Killkyle'!

I don't know which is the more trying, a holiday at a home which winds up as a grand advice centre, or a 'holiday' abroad which is one of Dad's preaching tours. One particular tour was scheduled during the summer months. In order to have at least a few weeks together Dad decided to bring the whole troop! It was our first journey to America. The boys were a year old, Cherith was a year and eleven months, I was eight and Sharon ten. My mother was either courageous or mad! We flew the Atlantic in a propeller plane, refuelling in Newfoundland. We flew into New York's JFK Airport but there was some sort of strike underway so we had to circle for a couple of hours. Then we landed and had to join the queue for a 'parking space' for two more hours. During our wait on the runway, the air conditioning system broke down so that the hostesses found it necessary to open the emergency doors to let in some 'fresh' air. The air was thick with the smell of fuel and the heat was incredible, but we all survived. Once off the aircraft we had a coach journey to take us to Cape May, New Jersey. The driver obviously wasn't too hot on directions and took us sixty miles the wrong way!

We reached Cape May at last and the Bible Convention got underway in fine style! First my mother broke a finger as a strong gust of wind blew the heavy hotel door closed on her hand. Then my younger sister, Cherith, decided to brave the swimming pool on her own; of course, it was irrelevant to a two-year-old that it would help to be able to swim. Since that day to this, I've been in some strange situations with Cherith, but I've never seen her upside down being resuscitated by an English nurse! We both agree that this was either the best favour the English have done for us, or else it was the worst!

Not to be outdone by all this attention, Kyle inflicted upon himself a nasty eye injury with a fork. He managed to scrape the retina of his eye and the doctor's advice included, ' . . . just as long as he is kept out of the sun' – dead simple in the middle of an American summer! Then to cap it all, the Irish lobby had to arrive to picket my father, and my mother was taking part in one of the conference witness programmes when the platform she had been on collapsed. It had been sabotaged – the stands had been sawn through to give way as the various representatives got on and off the thing. So much for Cape May.

Holidays provided time to meet our cousins who lived some distance away. My cousin Alison and I weren't, for most of the time, exactly what you would term young ladies and forever there were tears of upset from Heather, her older sister, and Sharon over our 'stupidity'. One day in particular, Sharon and Heather appeared in the kitchen most annoyed and very embarrassed and asked to speak privately to Mummy. Alison and I were summoned immediately:

'OK you two – go and remove it.' Poor Mum was obviously having difficulty not seeing the funny side yet she had complete sympathy with Sharon and Heather. We ran upstairs falling all over each other in our laughter to remove 'it'. 'It' was Sharon's first bra which we had made into a flag to deck the wall outside her bedroom window!

Those sensitive days of early womanhood for Sharon and Heather certainly were not eased by their two younger, less mature sisters. The finest moments of friendship for Alison and me were when we were away from the sensible and protective eyes of Heather and Sharon, for then our 'stupidity' had free range – often to our detriment, mind you.

I suppose one of the grandest holidays we ever enjoyed was that which was given to us as a present from our congregation. It was a gift to the family to mark my father's fortieth anniversary as their minister. Their kindness in including us all in this way will not be forgotten. Isn't it strange how at a moment of achievement there is always someone who has to winge? Not long after we had received this gift, I heard about a person who was displeased about such a gesture and found reason for it in the fact that this was a gift from the church and therefore a misuse of God's money. Now they never did say anything straight to any of our family so either it was hearsay or the person wasn't being quite so honest herself by not saying openly to those whom it concerned what their view was. At any rate, they are welcome to their view on how 'God's money' should be spent. I tend to feel a workman is worthy of his hire and I had to really laugh when a few months later I heard that this same critic was off on a holiday themselves with a member of the opposite sex and both single! I couldn't help but wonder which had the better appearance – God's people spending God's money on God's man, or two single people of the opposite sex heading off to a beachy resort alone! To me there is nothing wrong with either, but surely in the light of the criticism levelled, the second had also to be taken into account! These wee legalistic niceties often have a rather neat way of judging themselves.

This holiday was taken by us during the summer months as that is always the most suitable for each of us to get time off. We began in Strasbourg, France, as Dad had to be there for the EEC Parliamentary Session and we planned to head straight on after its close. My father's assistant, Councillor Nigel Dodds, and his wife, Diane, had similar plans to begin their holidays after the session, so they and their baby son, Mark, joined us that week. My sister's little girl, Lydia, is only older than Mark by a few months and there was instant fun there. Most of the humour was along political lines for the rest of us as the atmosphere of the parliament lent itself to that. We were all enjoying a delicious meal in the dining room there – the choice and variety of the food was excellent – and as we were talking together afterwards and waiting for our coffee, my brother Ian (whose appetite is amazing) looked over to Dad and in mock seriousness said, 'Well, Dad, one thing I can say – the anti-Christ sure knows how to set up a meal!'

After that week Nigel, Diane and Mark headed off to the west and we to the south. For two weeks we enjoyed perfect weather and after a couple of vain attempts by a journalist or two, we also enjoyed perfect peace from the media. Those days were the most refreshing I believe we have known as a family. We had time to be together, time and freedom from the usual security precautions to be alone, and time to take off when and whenever without having to make arrangements. At the close of our second week, a friend of ours, Bobby Jones, met up with us. He is the grandson of Dr Jones, Jr. and is the same age as Ian and Kyle – well, one day older. He then travelled with us into Italy where in Milan we had a rendezvous with Dr and Mrs Jones Jr. and Bobby's parents, the Jones IIIs. For the next few days, Italy was taken by storm. Milan, Genoa, Turin, Florence and finally Rome. At the end of those days another fortnight at the beach would not have come in amiss. France I love and always have since my first visit to it. Italy? Well, Italy was, let us say, an experience.

Everywhere we went there were masses of tourists all gulping in the famed art works, cathedrals and landmarks. Frankly, that sort of a holiday holds no appeal for me. The poor souls all looked haggard and sweaty as they queued for hours to get into these various museums. At least the places we chose we managed to schedule at times least demanded, albeit at the crack of dawn. In France all of us knew a smattering of the language and communication was no problem. In Italy not one of us knew the lingo and the laughs we had certainly made our ignorance worthwhile. Dad, at first, was of the mind that if he spoke a good deal slower and considerably louder, he would be understood. Another member of our little tour group thought by repeating everything just the same only with accompanying actions, the matter would be solved. Eventually we got through to Dad that a different pace and volume really wasn't the answer. So, the next time, he said everything in English with an Italian accent. Now this could well have worked but we never found out because we were all laughing so hard.

Travelling with Dad has its advantages. One of our trains was halted and half of the travellers told to get off. Not speaking Italian, we, of course, hadn't a clue as to the reason, which turned out quite simply to be that a restaurant car was being added to the centre of the train for the remaining journey.

'This is ridiculous,' said Dad. 'Our tickets are supposed to be direct – there's nothing about changing halfway. I'm going to talk to one of these men. Come on with me, Rhonda.' Off we set, leaving the others sitting between the tracks on top of all our cases. Talking as though the wee guard was his own police escort, Dad said,

'Look, Sir, we have tickets here to take us direct to Milan and now we are all abandoned with no indication as to where we are to get our connection.' Typically Italian, the guard shrugged his shoulders, pouted his mouth and mumbled some gibberish.

'Huh!' said Dad. 'He'll understand this.' Out came Dad's EEC passport and membership card. 'My name is Ian Paisley, and I am a member of the EEC Parliament and this is no way to treat travellers,' said Dad somewhat more assertively now, and somewhat more guard-like, the wee man straightened himself, read the name again, and through enlarged eyes, looked again at Dad and saluted.

'This way, Sir,' he said in English, and our problem was solved.

In one of the museums we visited, Dad was standing back taking in a large oil painting. He was totally wrapped up in its message and obviously deep in thought. I began walking towards him from the other side of the gallery only to behold a smallish lady in the process of walking round Dad, staring as if he was one of the exhibits also. I paused to take in this little scene. Walking away from Dad – eyes still fixed on him – she nudged a nearby man, presumably her husband:

'That's Ian Paisley!' she said in an English accent.

'Never!' he replied. 'Ian Paisley in Italy? Never!'

'It is, I heard him talking in the last room and now I've had a good look. It *is* him'.

The man moved closer, squinting his eyes as he neared Dad, who was still totally oblivious to their gaze. He stopped abruptly, eyes de-squinted now, as though he'd seen a ghost. He turned back to the woman:

'Well I never, it is him!'

Dad was now ready to move on. For a second his eyes met

theirs, he nodded and smiled, having heard nothing of their conversation, and went on his way. I thought I should have to tackle the task of scraping their wilted bodies off the wall!

Italy too had its depressing side. For a Protestant by faith it is remarkably hard to watch people prostrate themselves before statues and crawl upon their knees in the way directed by their Church. To listen to the repetition of rosaries and see hands rub their fingers over strings of beads all in pursuit of eternal peace and forgiveness of sins is a pitiable sight when the faith you hold is not built upon such superstitions or works for justification.

The contrast of beliefs between the Protestant faith and the Roman Catholic Church is what I shall most remember from my visit to Italy. The Church is rich in its art works, and in the sheer magnitude of its buildings. They are in their own way and scale awe-inspiring, but it is a purely material inspriation without eternal permanence or hope. Knowing that salvation is a free gift and Christ alone can mediate between God and man turns the 'inspiration' of Rome into a cold-hearted and callous racket responsible for taking money for the redemption of souls, which it cannot deliver.

As I walked through these great cathedrals and through the breathtaking beauty of the Vatican and looked at tokens of man's work, such as the Cistine Chapel, my own faith became more real to me than before; real in the sense that for the first time art, the subject which has brought to my life much joy and a unique dimension of love and friendship with Christ, stood before me in all its pomp and magnificence as a *replacement* for Christ in worship instead of an additional aid. The second Commandment struck me with full force and I felt for the first time the grip that idolatry establishes. I had understood in my head the reasons for such a Commandment as this, but the heart-pull of idolatry and its earthly comforts had never tugged at me before. I could see why idolising something material, something which could actually be touched, had an appeal and a comfort. Perhaps my interest in and love of art played the heart-feelings louder to me, perhaps not, but whatever the cause the teaching of the second Commandment became real in a new way. Idolatry for the Protestant is usually placing something in their lives above Christ, so the literal meaning of this Commandment is seldom appreciated these days, since idols and icons are not used in Protestant churches. It has a strange thing to grasp the literal meaning of a scriptural teaching so late in the day, having applied its implications to my life for many years.

After the hectic days we spent in Italy it was bliss to sit quietly during the two-hour flight to London, being spoken to in English and offered something other than spaghetti to eat. But the bliss didn't last long. There was no mistaking the fact that we were going back to the same old Ulster when we boarded our flight to Belfast, since there was some security hitch and the plane had to be unloaded of its luggage, each passenger had to identify their cases lined up along the runway, and one hour late we hit the clouds for Belfast. It had been a terrific holiday, but it couldn't last forever – home and back to everything it meant to be a Paisley. Often on returning to Ulster I wonder if I shouldn't just gather up my belongings and stay away!

CHAPTER EIGHT

I Believe in Angels

'The Angel of the Lord encampeth round about them that fear
him and delivereth them.'

This seventh verse of Psalm 34 has over many years been
proved to my family. Belief in angels brings courage, encouragement, peace and comfort. I believe in angels.

There is not a day that passes which does not bring with it
the possibility of death for any of us. In Ulster the ongoing
situation underscores this reality. The thought that my father
could be murdered comes often to my mind. Like all fears
there are occasions when it takes on a colossal guise. The fear
must be met, not avoided. It must be faced and not just hidden
for a while by human reasoning. This I can assure you is easier
said than done!

Now, for goodness sake don't let me give you the impression
that each day I or anyone in my family sit anxiously waiting
for bad news. We don't. For a start, work is too demanding
for such luxury, and secondly, the relationship with Christ in
each of our lives provides a means of overcoming fear. The
whole security issue is one which my brothers, sisters and I
grew up with. For this reason personal security is not a matter
of unusual concern. It always existed and sometimes looks as
though it always will! Concern for Dad is different and indeed
concern for other friends and colleagues is the same. The
vulnerability of a person whom you know and love is often
more apparent than your own.

There have always been men on duty at our home. I cannot recall the first day they came on duty and so for us security is a way of life. You can therefore understand why simply walking alone or heading somewhere away from 'eyes' with a friend is not just a pleasant interlude but a necessary release valve!

As Dad became active in Ulster's developing situation he became more and more a target – for the various Republican movements, for the inevitable nutcases, for Protestants who were vehement in their opposition to him, and on occasions for authorities in power who would have been happier if he wasn't alerting our province to their cunning and betrayal.

At first it was the old 'B Specials' who guarded the house. Our previous home was attacked several times and the only protective arrangements provided for these men was a pile of sandbags around our gate! Dad opened the garage for them as it was much more secure and commanded a good view of our house and garden. These men were excellent playmates for five youngsters. They had a never-ending supply of sweets and joined in every game from football to the burial services of our pets. Some of these men are still known to us and we hold them in high esteem.

When the Specials were disbanded their duties passed on to the RUC Reserve Force. Again, many of these men we have got to know well over the years and they have become good friends of the family. We remain indebted to them for the work which they do.

The men who escort Dad on a daily basis are of course better known to us. We know them as part of the family, and while their wives and children are not as well known to us, they are often in our thoughts and prayers. The escorts have long hours for my father is a busy man. I am sure that at times their wives must get fed up and wish they were doing some other job.

Of all their duties, I believe the one they must detest the most is covering the early morning prayer meetings which Dad frequents. I used to attend these meetings on a regular basis. It was at one of these meetings that an attempt was carried out to shoot Dad. It wasn't by any means the first attempt on

Dad's life, but it was the closest I have ever been to someone seeking to harm him.

For Dad not to be present at one of these meetings is a rare exception, but on that morning his plans had been altered. I was coming out of the meeting about fifteen minutes before it was due to close just as a car drove into the car park. It stopped very close to me, parallel to my own car. I was unlocking my door and remember being surprised by the nearness of the car. There were three men in it. The front passenger swung his door open with one hand, the other was tucked inside his lapel. He was wearing black leather gloves and a dark raincoat. The back passenger had already got half way out of the far side.

'Is Paisley in there this morning?'

'No, he's not,' I replied.

The man from the back seat got back in and the other began to close the front door. The back passenger called out, 'Is he not praying today?' and laughed the coldest laugh I have ever heard. It wasn't a cynical laugh, nor a laugh of unbelief, nor even of mockery. It was the laugh of disappointed hatred.

The car swung around and drove at speed out of the grounds. This whole incident was very brief and I got into my car and headed on to work. But as I drove it replayed across my mind; the black gloves, the unknown car, the question, the laugh, and I realised that these men had meant business. I rang home, Dad answered and I told him what had happened. He agreed it was suspicious, said he would be careful, told me not to worry and decided he would let his escorts know straight away. Before the morning had passed the Irish National Liberation Army – INLA – had issued a statement saying they had attempted to shoot Dad and that he remained on their hit list.

The day's activities went on. We all carried out our duties. Bids had been made on Dad's life before. We were thankful for God's protection yet again over someone we cherish dearly, but life doesn't stop. It cannot, for in many ways that would be to allow such occurrences victory.

As I got into bed that night, however, and as the days happenings walked through my mind again, the fact that I had actually spoken to the men who intended to kill my father really hit me! I had stood close to them, I could have reached out and touched them! They had come to take Dad away from us – a dear and kind father and a loving husband . . . but what did all that count for in their world of hatred and murder? It was a strange overcast feeling that invaded my bedroom that night, heavy and frightening.

The time got to about two or three a.m. I got up, opened my curtains and sat on the window seat looking out into the clear morning at the big elm tree in our front garden, and then beyond – over the rooftops and across the city centre. How I wished for a vocabulary that could express to Christ the depth of my thankfulness for keeping Dad safe. All I could say was 'O God', and without warning hot tears burned their way down my face.

I cried for a long time that night. I remembered with pity the homes in Ulster broken by the men of violence. I had never felt like this about the plight of our province before.

I do not write this to prove that I have a great sentiment for Ulster. Often my cynicism and hardness over the situation disgusts me. I suppose it is all a matter of survival, and a degree of resilience is necessary in a place like this. That night, perhaps it was because death seemed actually personified I wished that somehow I possessed the ability to love and to heal the broken-hearted. I have tried to maintain something of that which swept its way into my soul in those quiet hours – surely it is a most vital part of living always to care for one another, to be as willing to share the distresses and burdens as we are the successes and joys of the normal events of life.

I did not feel I had got anywhere that night. The men's illogical and irrational behaviour, the devastation of so many years, the hopelessness of tomorrow – all these clamoured for my attention. There was so much, and all I could say was 'O God'. Helplessness stared back at me and I crawled back under the bedcovers to get warm and to let sleep still the demands on my mind.

I did not say anything about being upset – frankly I felt a bit daft about it and rationally and spiritually inadequate. In fact, it was not until some weeks later, while Dad was preaching and was illustrating a point in his evening sermon, that I understood what I had felt. He was telling the story of a man who had been praying for a specific thing for a long time. The man was a minister, and Dad recorded how the request weighed on his mind to such an extent one evening that all he could do was to pray 'My God'. The illustration coloured instantly. Christ knows, I thought, how futile was my search for words! He knows better than I can say it anyway. The pleasure of allowing this insight to embrace me was as beautiful and comforting as being cuddled by someone I loved.

Not many days later in my Bible readings I read: 'The Angel of the Lord encampeth round about them that fear him and delivereth them'. To this day I find numerous comforts from this promise, and I claim it for many friends and loved ones. The angels' wings, in their guardian role, I am confident will not be folded to rest until God himself chooses to free the temple of his Spirit which they guard from the dangers of this world. And then, only then, will he give the grace to accept his decision.

Attempts on Dad's life have been made since then, and numerous threats have been issued, and I forget my promise when fear stalks in. But God reminds me faithfully, and I must consciously lift my eyes to His landscape.

Like everything that is part of daily living, security matters are not noticed by us most of the time. They exist and will continue. Often it is only humour which brings them to our attention. Late one Saturday we were sitting around talking and suddenly a shot rang out. Immediately Dad switched out the lights and spoke through our intercom to the police outside.

'Are you men all right? Hello, men. Are you OK?'

No reply.

'Och, that thing's so unreliable,' Dad remarked, 'you wouldn't know whether or not it's coming through.'

Meanwhile my mother's curiosity had got the better of her and taken her to the back porch, where she was peering through the curtains.

'Ian, the men are moving about, so everything must be OK. Maybe it wasn't a shot after all.'

'I know a shot when I hear one,' retorted Dad. He opened the door and went out. 'Keep inside,' he told my brothers.

A few minutes later Dad came back in.

'No trouble. The landrover's there – apparently one of the guns went off by accident. Dear help the fella, I'm sure he'll have to explain how it happened.'

A week or so later we learned exactly how the accident happened. A dozy inspector decided to approach our driveway quietly in order to check that the men were patrolling properly. The men heard something and challenged. Not content that he had his proof, he moved forward. The man on duty prepared his weapon – obviously in the wrong way – and it went off, the bullet embedding itself in the pathway inches from the inspector's feet. The inspector dropped on the spot and wet himself! The poor man was suffering from nervous exhaustion, hence his bad judgement, and he was put on the sick, while the guy with the gun was sent back to retrain in weaponry!

There have been a number of MI5 controversies over their involvement in discrediting Ulster politicians, among them Dad. On one occasion a file they had compiled of our family, home, etc. complete with photographs, had to be handed over. During one such controversy Dad had been drawing attention to what was going on, and as usual in Ulster, and especially in our household, many jokes resulted. Early one morning Cherith, Ian and I set out with Mum. She was driving, and a blue car appeared to be tailing us. After taking the same turn as us for the fourth time Mum remarked,

'I hope they aren't tailing us'. Ian responded,

'Never worry, Ma, it's probably just the MI5!' Two minutes later they took a different turning and he concluded, 'There you are. They must have heard!'

Security measures are always being reviewed. Not long ago there was a big reassessment of Dad's security, both personal and on the house. There had been much controversy over the Anglo-Irish Agreement and threats at the time were fourteen to the dozen. All the bullet-proof windows were removed and replaced with ones of a better quality. Various other measures were taken, and this included the erection of a new type of gate.

For this monstrosity each of us was issued with a remote control unit. Unfortunately, the gate caused numerous problems and the authorities were trying desperately to iron them out. For example, it jammed closed one lunchtime and Dad had to climb over it to get out to a radio interview. They jammed half shut on another occasion and our cars had to be abandoned half-way down the drive and out into the road.

Late one night Ian, Cherith and I arrived home from a party and were in a jovial mood. Everyone else was out. The policeman who let us in remarked,

'I see the gate seems to be working OK now'.

'Don't speak too soon,' one of us replied laughingly. The three of us looked at each other, knowing full well what each was thinking.

'Come on,' said Ian, holding aloft his remote control unit, 'let's have a laugh with this thing.' We headed upstairs to a window in direct line with the gate and out of view from the security hut.

Flick and the gate began to open. Two policemen stepped out into the path.

'How did that happen? Did you knock the switch?'

'I wasn't near it. You maybe tapped it yourself.'

'Maybe I did. Better shut it.'

The gate began to close. *Flick* It stopped half-way. Out came the two men again.

'What happened there?'

'That gate is more trouble than it's worth.'

'Better go down and take a look.'

They dandered down the path, no doubt chittering about its worthlessness. Half-way down, Ian flicked the control again and the gate began to close. They stood still in complete shock. By now they were too far away to hear. They walked on towards the closed gate. As one bent down to examine the control box, Ian flicked his unit again and the policemen jumped back in horror.

By this time the three of us were in convulsions. It was the

Top: Dad and Bishop as a pup. **Bottom:** January 1988: Sharon and John with Lydia.

Top: Dad on the campaign trail! **Bottom:** June 1986 - June 1987: The first official photograph of our year in office.

Dad enjoying a parade in Derry.

Dad and I on the chat show 'Saturday Live'.

'change of guard' who caught us out. As the relief vehicle drew up they spied the ray of light from the window. The two men were 'well had' as the saying goes. We hurried down and had a laugh with them all – just to keep ourselves right!

The new windows caused less bother – except for one in the entrance porch. Dad was leaving for his morning's work when he noticed that a pane of it was shattered in lines outwards from a central hole about the size of a ball-bearing.

'You'd nearly think that was from an airgun pellet,' he said to the escort. They laughed at the thought of this.

'Better have one of the men look at it,' replied the escort, and called over the policeman on duty who was a new face and a self-opinionated wee pup. After removing his cap and peering at the hole he stated knowledgeably:

'It looks as though the heat we have been having has shattered that.'

There was utter silence! I looked at Mum and said, 'You want to see the way they've melted upstairs,' and we burst out laughing.

It's a good job we don't depend on man's security systems. Of course security is an important and necessary part of life, but I firmly believe that it needs to be kept in healthy perspective. The wickedness of men is far keener in its evil creativeness than any ring of security, with all its ingenuity. Having trusted Christ with the security of my soul for eternity, I have to learn to entrust to him the earthly lives of those I love dearly.

For this reason I always fail to understand why so many Christians support the arms race. To pour such wealth into an unnecessary means of destruction is horrific. Already there are enough destructive forces to annihilate this planet. The superpowers have defence in abundance, as do the minor powers. How can we watch scenes of famine on television and justify this false balance of expenditure? How can we look at slum areas and inner cities and nod approvingly at the development of more missiles with greater ability to wipe out more human life? How can we see the deterioration of finances for health and education and not oppose the build up of force? How can we look at the thousands unemployed and see possible revenue for job creation channelled to nuclear weaponry?

We must not look without questioning. Defence is necessary I am told. Agreed. Nature, history and experience teach us the wisdom of preparation against predators. But what we have today is not the wisdom of defence. It is the folly of an obsession for self-preservation at too high a cost.

It is time for God's children to lead by example and voice their concern at the exploitation of the needy in the cause of so–called defence. God expects us to be cautious and wise in our dealings one with another as nations. He also requires that wisdom is rooted in him. He is the source of all power and all love. 'Thy gentleness has made me great,' the psalmist wrote. Caution tempered with gentleness brings honesty. World politics is deceptive and based on man's knowledge. It is impure, but the wisdom from God is 'first pure, then peaceable, gentle and easy to be intreated, full of mercy and good fruits, without partiality and without hypocrisy' (James 3:17). I have often heard that politics is the art of compromise, but I have observed that the further the compromise is from high moral values and scriptural ideals, the more people talk about 'a good, sensible, practical politician'. You also have a discontented nation where the rich do get richer, the poor do get poorer, and a world which reverberates with hatred and distrust.

In Ulster it is easy to forget world politics and the huge problem of world security. We may be just a tiny province, but our festering wound of the past twenty years makes us oblivious to that fact. It fools us into thinking that the rest of the world sees our need.

The truth is, it does not. When all is said and done, Ulster counts for precious little as far as the British Government and every other government is concerned. Is it wise to depend on them for security? I think not. If a government is not trustworthy over a small province, is it likely to be more so in world affairs? No, I see no safeguard over my heritage under Britain. I see it only under Ulstermen who have a vested interest in the province's future. Likewise I can find no evidence of care for this earth's preservation among powers and superpowers. Instead, I find it among God's children who take seriously the responsibility given to them in Genesis to subdue it and have dominion over it. Dominion brings under control earth's resources, and we should be subduing them for the benefit and well-being of all peoples.

Dad does not place his daily security in the hands of any police force, no matter how much he respects the rank and file of it. He has not let attempts against his life shroud his nature in resentment and bitterness. He seeks to live gently for and with his fellow men. I realise as his daughter that this might not accord with his public image, but you must give some credence to those who follow him and support him and know him – and not believe all you have read in the past.

Every morning he prays faithfully for God's protection over the men who are on duty with him and over his colleagues and himself. His prayers have been heard and his faithfulness in this matter often rebukes my carelessness. His concern for those in political life as well as for the ordinary citizen and members of the security forces is evidenced by his efforts to have security in this province placed in the hands of those who understand the situation here, namely, Ulstermen. Dad is, in that way, security-conscious and he is aware of the danger he lives in, but he is by no means 'hyper' about the matter and, indeed looks forward to the day when personal security is no longer necessary. I cannot foresee that day even in my most optimistic moments!

In the meantime, having security men around has its uses. Our dog – to whom you will be introduced later in this book – is quite a character. The brute would have to be, to survive in our household! Anyway, he had annoyed a moan of a woman who lived a road or two away from us and she decided one day to take him hostage. She came round to our house and tore strips off the policemen on duty, as none of us were in! That night it was about 10.30 when we began arriving home from various meetings and learned of the 'dog-napping'.

'Right,' said Dad, 'She's no business taking our dog. She can report us to whoever she wishes, but she can't have Bishop.

I'm going to get him girls,' he said, looking at Cherith and me who had been encouraging him. 'Are you coming?'

Our coats were already on! The three of us set off down the path and as Dad's men had already been dismissed leaving only those on duty guarding the house, one of them came with us. Picture it – Ian Paisley and a uniformed RUC man equipped with machine gun, and two giggling daughters out in search of a dog.

We walked down the street we believed the woman lived in and began calling softly, 'Bishop! Here boy!' and Dad whistled his familiar summons for the dog. Soon we heard him barking – the dog that is – and lo and behold a door and then a gate opened and closed and dear old Bishop came rejoicing up the street to meet us. Freed! The four of us just stood and laughed. I looked at Dad and the armed policeman and said,

'Well, I wouldn't say she'd been intimidated or anything!' When we arrived back home, Mum said in amazement,

'That didn't take long – what happened?'

'He just reappeared,' replied Dad.

'The Third Force arm bands, the balaclavas and the machine gun might have helped a little,' Cherith and I laughed. We agreed it was a classic case of police harassment.

Perhaps the greatest intrusion of personal security is felt by Mum and Dad in their private life. It is impossible for them to head out for a quiet drive together or for a walk by themselves, for example, or even go out for a meal without others being present. No matter how unobtrusive, they are still there.

My father has been involved in activities to which he would not have his escorts bring him. It is not his wish at such times to embarrass them, nor place them in an awkward position. One night Dad had such an engagement – a meeting to plan a forthcoming protest rally – and as my car was the only one free he asked me to be his driver. Ian and Cherith were at home and decided to come along too.

Poor Dad's patience was tried as the three of us threw ourselves enthusiastically into the role of secret agents with a large object to get undetected past two policemen and two full-beam security lights and through the notorious gate. For a laugh my brother appeared with some shoe polish and offered to make Dad up! We eventually got out of the house unnoticed with Dad. Half serious, yet unable to keep a straight face, he lectured us on the importance of the situation:

'This is no laughing matter. You're a bunch of mockers, that's what you are. If I'd known you were going to behave like this I'd have driven myself.'

By now he was safely into the back seat of my two-door car with my brother beside him, ordering us all out of existence. Ian threw a rug over Dad and pulled his head down onto his knee (to a muffled cry of protest from Dad) and I drove out onto the road. Cherith and I were giggling like two six-year-olds and when Dad surfaced for air all he could do was laugh as well. We made the rendezvous in perfect time and Dad headed to this meeting in more sedate company, I can assure you. I thought, when the history of Ulster is written, the real truth will never be known!

One night prior to this, Dad and some other activists in the Party (not that there are anything but activists in the DUP) had arranged to carry out a poster campaign over the border in Dublin. The posters read 'Ulster is British' and were to be hung at several strategic points in the city. Again we were conscripted to provide transportation to the meeting point – Mum, Cherith and me this time. Buckets and paste brushes were being packed into the two cars which were being used as we arrived with Dad and Mr Peter Robinson whom we had collected en route. Those involved were behaving like excited schoolboys heading off on a trip. A couple of them had brought some food for the journey and one was clad in tinted glasses and a hat by way of disguise. He looked so daft that it was one way of getting attention rather than avoiding it!

Dad gave Mum a kiss on the cheek.

'See you in the morning, dear.'

'You men be careful,' she responded.

'Have you ever known me to be anything else, dear?' he asked patronisingly.

'Yes,' said Mum and they laughed.

'Goodbye girls, and behave,' said Dad.

'Have you ever known us to do anything else?' we choroused.
'Yes,' came the reply of course.

A couple of minutes, a few roars of laughter and their cars
were away. We drove home quietly, wondering if all would
go well. It did. They made it to Dublin, hung their posters
and were home by morning to hear the news headlines carry
the story of their protest.

The best part of any such exploit in Ulster is when everyone
returns afterwards, the kettle goes on and the event is retold.
Usually this happens around our kitchen table. One point of
Dad's account of that night still makes me laugh. When the
car was stopped at a border checkpoint the Guards on duty
looked in and after the routine questions asked, 'What is the
purpose of your visit?' 'Tourism,' was the reply. 'OK, on your
way.' Tourism – at 2 a.m.!

The second incident was that of the guy on duty at one of
the locations marked for postering who said when he saw Dad
approach him,

'Och, is it yourself, Mr Paisley?' and proceeded to open the
gate! He never asked about the bucket of paste he was carrying
– nor about the friends armed with ladders and posters!

You can, I hope, understand that if we were to allow security
to become a major issue of concern in our lives, we would
never get a day's peace nor a refreshing night of sleep! Christ's
guardianship has to be the place where trust is laid. When the
situation becomes more tense, as it does very often, the laughs
are few and the atmosphere broods like a cat of prey – all claws
and vindictive in spirit. Release from the heavy, pressured
weight of the problem comes when I think of the kindly wings
of protection and even I can soar above the turmoil to find
pleasant solace. 'Underneath and round about are the ever-
lasting arms.'

CHAPTER NINE

You Can Tell a Man By His Friends

'You can tell a man by his friends.' Adhering to this, it is reasonable to assume that the choice of a man's best friend reveals most about him. Dad's best friend is his wife – something which I am continually learning is not always the case in life. Having been raised in a home where my parents' closeness to one another was always apparent, it was easy for me to assume that that was what marriage was all about. My parents have their moments of aggro with one another like all people do. But I can honestly write that I have never witnessed them fight and row with one another, nor treat the other in a manner which is demeaning or hurtful. The mutual respect which they hold for each other has granted us, their children, the privilege and security of seeing by example a successful marriage at work. They joke and tease and have differences of opinion. They give and take. Unselfishly, they desire the best for one another and their children. Companionship and complete trust is how I can best summarise their friendship.

With divorce continuing to increase, with unfaithfulness to the marriage covenant, and with illicit love as it is today, it is no wonder that the joy has gone out of so many lives. The shattering of this covenant trust is of such magnitude that only Christ has the power to restore people's ability to trust each other. Forgiveness is not the solution to the problem, for when a person loves, they can easily forgive even the sorest wound. It is the foundation of trust that is so difficult to rebuild – trust in one's own judgement and trust in others. Trust means in many ways a willingness to be vulnerable.

My work takes me into various situations among believers and unbelievers. Often when at meetings where both are present, many of them married men, the conversation turns to the opposite sex. The number of married men with their eye on someone else did have me a little taken aback at first, I must admit. I wasn't totally shocked or surprised, for we were never raised aloof from the realities of life. I just never thought so many were into it! However, what I have to admit was my amazement when the same attitude and talk about women came from those professing Christ as their Saviour! It seemed the norm to join in deciding who would be 'OK' for a night! In many cases I am sure it was nothing more than talk, but it reflected a poor picture of marriage as ordained by their Lord. I wondered how my feelings of friend, or lover, or my self-image would have been affected had I been the wife. I know women can be just as guilty; it's just that I haven't come across it very much myself because women are a minority in the work I do.

The opposite to this secular male is the male chauvinism of which I'm afraid only Christians can be guilty. You know the type of male zealot I mean – he phones up to ask you out and begins,

'I've been praying about asking you out and God has shown me that I should'. I suppose the trick here is to embarrass out of you an 'Oh, I'd love to go, then'.

Funny thing is, it doesn't seem to matter to him if God has given you the opposite message!

Not long ago a friend of mine was telling me about one of these cases who proposed to her. He had never shown her any affection beyond that of a good friend. He arrived at her house one Christmas and gave her a ring:

'Here you are,' he said, 'God has shown me I'm to marry you.'

'Really, I couldn't wear that,' she replied, quite alarmed by this outburst. 'I don't feel our friendship is quite what you think and besides, I really don't want to marry you.'

'Take it,' he responded. 'I have a verse for giving it to you. When you get a verse telling you otherwise, I'll take it back.' She had more sense than to submit to such reasoning.

Submission is a two-way thing. Mum and Dad are pretty good at it. The ease with which their lives run together is the fruit of submissiveness. You know, sometimes I have to laugh to myself when I see Mum get excited about Dad arriving home or when Dad comes in saying 'Where's your mother?' without so much as a 'Hello' first. I laugh, not in mockery but just at the sheer happiness of seeing my parents behaving like teenagers over one another's company. They are infatuated with each other and it is a warming peace for a child to share the contentment of their parents, no matter what political storm is raging outside the home.

My father is a total romantic and Mum loves it. Mind you, she is as gone as he is. They believe in a romance that I must admit lies outside my own experience. Dad knows this and always responds,

'Rhonda, someday you will believe!' So far I haven't been convinced!

Romance for me is a momentary thing in time. Its meaning and beauty form terrific and inspiring memories. More often it is when I am alone, but sometimes it has been in someone's company. I walked in a snowfall once with a dear friend of several years' standing. It was on a Sunday in January and the fallen snow lay about a foot deep. All noise had been muffled into tenderness and the air was perfectly calm. Large snowflakes fell slowly, dreamlike over us as we talked and laughed and loved. The romance of that moment I shall never lose. Its peace often inspires me.

On an early spring afternoon I walked along a beach with a friend, and a stray dog adopted us as his playmates. In and out of the sea he splashed, rescuing sticks. The colour, light and joy of those hours still touches its romance on my heart. My friend was a musician and songwriter, and he captured the moments in a more tangible way afterwards.

I played leapfrog with a friend on the firm sand near the water's edge when summer was coming and the sky sang out

a long bright night with its blazing sunset. I knew its romance
and it became part of my being. While the summer took with
her her nights, she couldn't take back time.

The romance of a split second in nature's beauty, then, is
what lifts my soul. Romance of this kind I can understand, but
the continuing romance which I see in my parent's lives is
beyond my comprehension, and, I believe, my ability.

The totality of their relationship spans every aspect of their
characters. They are one, yet neither has lost their individuality.
So many couples seem either to retain their individuality at the
cost of their marriage, or else one becomes an insipid half of a
so-called partnership. Getting and maintaining the balance
means hard work. My parents work well together. They share
and communicate. They don't treat anything to do with one
another as a burden or an unwanted responsibility.

Often Dad says to Mum as he heads out the door on another
preaching tour or on political business,

'I'll miss you dear, but we'll have all of heaven together'. At
such times I couldn't give a fig about heaven – I just want Dad
to be around a bit more now. Then I see Mum reach back in
response to his kiss and agree with him, totally happy at this
prospect, and I feel my lack of ability to understand this bond
which they share.

Fraternal love is as strong in their relationship as the romantic
kind, that is why they remain close and interesting to each
other. I believe that the Scriptures teach the combination of
these two types of love for a husband and wife. My mother
did not have the word 'obey' in her marriage vows, since there
is really no need for such a statement when each partner's heart
and mind are united in respect and love. Besides, I know that
the foundations of my parents' friendship is laid in their kinship
with Christ. This is the aspect of their relationship which has
left the deepest impression on me. Its greatest asset is that
you find yourself sharing your most joyful moments with the
personification of Infinity.

I am glad my parents have the friendship and love which
they do. It would be a much more difficult job for Dad if his
wife were a moan or a nag, and it would be impossible for

Mum if Dad were the dictator which many describe him as. Dad is in fact not bad around the house. I have seen him very occasionally with a vacuum cleaner, and the pace he can set with that machine is frightening. He does the odd bit of cooking and what he presents is tasty enough – if you can be content to eat it with so many dishes, pans and utensils on display! He always carves the Sunday roast, one of his finest culinary skills – but as a vegetarian I do not benefit from his art!

He is also a 'raker' when he has a bit of time on his hands, teasing and trying to get you going on something out of sheer devilment. With me and my sister, Cherith, it is vegetarianism, though just between you and me we have made a little impact there, because there are a couple of days in the week now when Dad doesn't have meat.

Generally speaking, there is not that much time when we are all together during the week. Sunday lunch is about the one time we can count on being together. Perhaps that's why we can all stand one another! It makes the time shared of greater value. Mum and Dad have a fast pace to their lives. They say it keeps them young. But now that they are getting older and we are all adults, nothing would make me happier than to see them enjoy more time with each other, doing all the things they have set to one side because of the responsibilities which they have undertaken. Frankly, I look forward to Dad's retirement from public life, although the longer I live the more I think I am deluding myself on that one!

Dad's fraternal friends are many and he alone has the right to name those he considers the closest. There are, however, some whose impact has been strongly felt by us as a family, and therefore I do not feel it out of place to mention a few of those whose lives have enriched and influenced us. I suppose that the number and variety of people coming in and out of our home is larger than the average household encounters. Our house, as far back as I can recall, was and continues to be the venue for meetings of all forms, shapes and sizes.

As a youngster the earliest I recall were the gatherings of student ministers late on Sunday nights. They would all drift in, in ones and twos, as their respective services ended and they arrived back in town. For the space of two hours the front bell jangled, signalling their arrival. Sharon and I were the only two children then and Mum had us already clad in pyjamas, slippers and dressing gowns. We were never sent on up to bed until we had seen all our 'uncles' and after our supper, before theirs began, we said our goodnights and were the recipients of numerous hugs.

The talk at first was usually quiet, as they wandered between the living room and the kitchen helping Mum with the supper and playing with Sharon and me, and telling one another about their meetings. Sharon was always in love with one of them! I think the longest-standing was Uncle Alan Cairns, whom she would inform us had lovely hair! As the night progressed things livened up, especially after Dad arrived home. At this point it was too late for little girls still to be up so we were given piggy-backs upstairs and bounced into bed with tremendous giggles. Well into the night we were aware of the deep male laughter from the kitchen below – the lull in noise while one voice spoke and then a mighty explosion of laughter and a gibberish of voices following. The play got tough sometimes in the early hours of the morning – after twelve midnight the first hours of Monday permitted these strict Sabbatarians to unleash their wit. There were several water fights I learned over the course of the months and a very famous ice-cube battle which put one of these young clerics backwards through a window!

These were the early days of the Free Presbyterian Church and knowing student ministers as friends who were fun-loving is something that not many children have the privilege of. The respect which we have for them now is deep. Having lived from childhood into adulthood parallel to the growth of the denomination is one of the greatest privileges I am sure I shall know. To see not just my father's ministry established but that of the Free Church grow to form over fifty congregations in Ulster, and others in Eire, England, Scotland, Australia, Canada, America and Spain is an experience which teaches much about the power of God versus the predictions of man.

The ministers and students now of the Free Church are much more numerous and many of them I know only by name. Our house would no longer hold them all on a Sunday night. Of those who were 'uncles' to Sharon and me and later to my younger sister and brothers, some stand out. Rev. Alan Cairns is now the minister of our church in Greenville, South Carolina. While I was a student he was my pastor – the only other I have had apart from Dad. He and his wife, Joan, showed me many kindnesses while I was away from home and their personal testimonies left a strong impression on my life. The ministry which Rev. Cairns presented each week was powerful in its theology yet tempered kindly with an abundance of Christ's love for the sinner. It was also refreshing to have a breath of Ulster humour so nearby when away from home.

Rev. Bert Cooke, the Deputy Moderator of the Free Church, and his wife, Agnes, were much loved by Sharon and me. Mrs Cooke is a kind and gentle lady and was always ready to amuse and talk to us. My mother has told me I was at one stage responsible for almost ending Rev. Cooke's ministry by giving him a heart attack. He was in our home and coming downstairs from my father's study. Our stairs were divided into two long flights with a little landing in between. I was about three years of age at the time and he had gone down the top flight when I came dandering along to the top of them. He stopped on the landing, reached out his hand and said,

'Are you coming, Rhonda?' Apparently I took him literally and jumped, landing with my arms around his neck. Mum said he appeared in the kitchen, where she was preparing a meal, looking as white as a sheet. I suppose the moral is never to ask or tell a Paisley to do anything for usually they take you at your word!

Then there were Rev. Ivan Foster and Rev. John Wylie. Somehow in my mind these two were always associated. I am sure the reason is because they were the two in prison at the same time as Dad. Uncle John Wylie was Best Man at my parents' wedding. Now that he is retired from preaching, he often attends our Sunday evening service and drops in for supper afterwards. He does still preach from time to time and

refers to himself as the 'spare-wheel' of the Free Church. Rev.
Foster is minister of the congregation at Kilskerry, County
Fermanagh, which was the first congregation of the Free
Church to open a day school. Both these men are highly
respected by my brothers, sisters and me. I think that the bond
which was created through the time of imprisonment is one
which I never will forget and always love them for – even
though on other matters we may not see eye to eye.

There are two other student ministers whom I remember
also. The first was Rev. William McCrea, now minister of
Magherafelt Church and Member of Parliament for Mid-
Ulster. He stayed in our home while a student minister. He is,
of course, also known widely as a gospel singer – what he is
known for in our house is something else! He was a great
carry-on and always having car accidents! His car was never
without a dent somewhere. He used to catch me as I slid down
the bannisters and then pretended to scold me when Mum
came running into the hall to see what the noise was. Now
that he has five kids of his own, he can, I am sure, understand
my mother's fears. Nowadays we always enjoy a bit of banter
about the Labour and Conservative parties. He favours the
latter in power, while I would prefer the former. He gets very
'into' the discussion just for the fun of it, and makes loud and
emotive speeches about it – even though we are only sitting in
an office. He is a great story teller too, about events he has
been in. In that respect he is very much like Dad and has, in
many ways, the same charisma as a politician that Dad has. In
Westminster I hear he is called 'the uncrowned prince'; I can
see why, although in Ulster I think the crown is his.

Finally, in my list of ministers, is Rev. David McIlveen, the
minister of Sandown Free Presbyterian Church and one of
Dad's associate ministers in our church. During Dad's second
imprisonment, he was very helpful to Mum where we were
concerned with lifts to and from school (Mum didn't drive at
that time) and arranging trips to the beach, etc. for us. He
remains a very close friend of our family and is like a son to
Dad. Falling between the religious and political fields is a dear
friend in London – Rev. Brian Green and his wife Pat, who

handles the DUP office in Westminster. Rev. Green I would say is one of Dad's closer close friends! His pastoral ministry in London is a source of much help to hundreds of people. As families we have always been close spending many holidays together along with their son, Nigel. During Dad's imprisonments Rev. Green often came to Belfast to help with much of the 'behind the scenes' work of the church. There would not be a week that passes that Dad and Brian Green are not in touch or together concerning business.

Completely away from the religious sphere, the other main area of friends, I suppose, is among our political colleagues. Naturally Dad's Deputy Leader, Mr Peter Robinson, is around quite a bit. He is totally different from Dad in his political style, which I think is a good thing for he would only be accused of mimicry otherwise. Media speculation from time to time mounts a neat little campaign suggesting Mr Robinson is forever waiting the moment to oust Paisley and seize control of the party. For the most part, these provide us all with a good laugh but it is nonetheless a hurtful way to get at a politician. What I have enjoyed most about my parents' friendship with Peter and his wife, Ins, is knowing their children. I feel they are little kindred spirits because of their father's position and the situation in the province. They are very loving children and each has a strong individual character. They will need it as children of a politician. As I look at them, I sometimes wish for their sakes they could stay young and innocent forever from Ulster's political awareness, but I have no doubt they will survive nobly.

The last of my father's friends whom I shall mention in this chapter falls neither into the political nor the religious fields. He is a Q.C. and while formerly a member of the old Stormont Parliament, he is no longer involved with any political aspect of life. He is the cleverest man I have ever met and yet the most humble. His name is Mr Desmond Boal and his professional standing is beyond reproof. He is extremely witty. Sharon and I, as children, only knew him as 'Pig Boal' – sounds awful but it was his own doing! He created a game with us whereby whoever sighted the other yelled, 'Pig!' For us, the yell was,

'Pig Boal!'; for him, 'Pigs!' How often we embarrassed our poor mother in the middle of town with that yell. And weird and wonderful were the looks Mr Boal got when he was first off the mark with 'Pigs!' My best description of him is that he is as eccentric as my father, and that is a compliment.

Having talked about pigs, now something about our dogs. We have never been without a pet dog. Our first dog was a cross between a Doberman and an Alsatian. He was jet black and his name was Captain. He was smart, alert and loving. He was the most sectarian animal I have ever known. Everybody took a great laugh out of teaching him tricks based on Dad's lingo. Captain could 'curse the Pope', give you his 'Protestant' paw and his 'Fenian' paw, and 'say his prayers'. For the most part, he was not politically motivated and joined in all the family's activities without prejudice!

He was a very obedient dog. He followed Dad everywhere and lay at his feet when he was reading or studying. In the end he had to be put to sleep. Dad had to take him to the vet because for a while he was sick and eventually we had to accept that it was kinder than to prolong his pain. We heard Dad's car drive up and Mum, Sharon and I ran to the door in the hope that Captain was back too. Mum opened the door and Dad was standing there, met by three pairs of hopeful eyes. All he could do was hold up the lead and say nothing. Sharon and I sat down on the stairs and cried as all children cry when their pets die. I wept more tears as a child over my beloved animals than I wish to recall – from frogs to tortoises to rabbits to dogs. I was always firmly of the opinion that they would be in heaven because they didn't know how to sin – such arguments I would get into with student ministers who frequented our house! My child's mind could not accept that they disintegrated and were no more, and if they were not in heaven, I reasoned, these men were saying they were in hell! To think of my poor pet rabbits or my blue budgie burning in hell was too much. Student ministers could be so stupid, I thought! My father had sense enough to comfort me and assure me that God would let them all rest, but he didn't mislead me.

'Won't they be in heaven now?' he always said,

'No dear, I don't think so, but they won't be disturbed,' and I was content to know they were not roasting over the devil's spit!

Captain was followed by Judy, an Alsatian. My mother was pregnant with Cherith at the time, and she and Dad were a little concerned that when the baby arrived the dog would be jealous. This never was the case. Judy proved to be the most gentle of all the dogs we have owned. Judy was our pet while Dad was in prison and she was an excellent guard dog, often arousing Mum during the night if a noise outside was heard. In fact, such was her zeal that a policeman, who decided to take a look around to make sure that everything was as it should be, was a victim of her teeth! During this time also, a lady who was a poodle breeder decided to give us a present of a puppy because she thought it would be something to cheer us up! It was a kind gesture and the little, black, curly mass of energy arrived. 'Sooty' was the name voted on by the five of us. We had the animal about a fortnight. One day, the pup was running around for all it was worth and then suddenly it stopped. There it was, lying in a heap – dead. Whether it died of sheer exhaustion, or twisted its neck, or because there was something wrong with it, we never knew. After a suitable period of mourning, Sooty II arrived and remained for many years. Judy mothered him and the two were inseparable. Sooty II was the only dog that tried my father's patience. He was such a small animal and constantly on the go. Truly I have never known an animal with such energy. He was forever around Dad's ankles, and between Dad trying to walk clear of the thing and Sooty tearing round his feet, it was a sight to behold!

By now Dad was busier than ever and his firm hand of discipline on our next dog was not as extensive as on the others. Jason was an Afghan hound. At the time of his arrival, there were several other pets besides Judy and Sooty: two rabbits, three tortoises, a gerbil and a hamster and, depending on the season, frogspawn, sticklebacks, etc. He fitted in immediately and accepted all the other pets. He was an absolute idiot! His obedience depended on his mood of the moment. 'Jason, sit!' and he would bound off in the opposite direction, his long legs lifting him high and fast, his coat rising and falling as though in slow motion. My father was the only one who could control him with due authority on a lead. When anyone else attempted to walk him, it became a case of their being dragged in every direction, Jason enjoying his ability to do so. Judy died of old age, Sooty was stolen during a spate of dog burglaries in our neighbourhood (much to the embarrassment of the police!), and then Jason had to be put to sleep because of sickness. As our other pets died over the course of the years, they were not replaced, but we did get another dog who is still on the scene. Dad took us all one Saturday morning to the USPCA kennels where we were going to look for a dog. He said that it would be better to first look here for some 'poor wee brute' who had been given a rough time, so we did.

There was a Border Collie who seemed to know he was up for sale and certainly didn't want to sell himself short – tail wagging and rubbing his head against us – begging to be wanted. He became ours and was christened Bishop – Bishop Paisley, just for the laugh of it! Bishop is a class dog. The weakness in his character is his insatiable desire for bitches! Now that he is older he is becoming somewhat more choosy and a little more sedate in his love-making, but for a time he seemed to be able to smell if there was a bitch on heat over a twenty-mile radius! For about the fourth time in the space of two days a wee grey-haired man came up the path with Bishop by the collar. It was my turn to be sent out to get the dog from him and apologise for his conduct (yet again) towards the man's animal on heat. This wee man wasn't too worried about the thing but faithfully brought Bishop back round home.

'Here he is again,' he laughed. 'Your Bishop is a right Casanova!'

'I know,' I laughed in response. 'He's well named.' I had it out before I realised it but he caught the humour and really chuckled. Unfortunately the policeman standing at my elbow did not, and if looks could kill, I would have been dead. I heard later that he was a member of the Church of Ireland!

It would be pleasant if in life dogs of the four-legged variety were the only ones we had to cope with – those of the two-legged breed are much more difficult to handle! While we have only had five of the former to cope with, the latter have been in great abundance. Dad has had so many confrontations I could never begin to record them all, nor do I wish to become personal about the matter but there are a few instances which are worth recollection.

Dogs of contention take various guises as far as Dad is concerned. The most on-going of these must be the press! When I was a youngster, I was convinced that 'the press' were totally sub-human, a race of monsters with gnashing pencils and spiral notepads. Anything about Dad in the papers in those days was pretty outrageous and the response often upon my ears was, 'Och, that's the press for you!' The press at home had a very bad image, I'm afraid. Have things changed?

My opinion of them in some instances has. With everything else, you have to take the good with the bad. There are several individuals in the press whom I have got to know through work and whom I respect – some others I have no esteem for and their journalism evidences their own prejudices.

There are many jokes based on Dad's rapport with the media. Possibly the best known one is that which happened when Dad was being interviewed one day and a rather ridiculous question was posed.

'Let me smell your breath,' came Dad's answer! Of course, there isn't a more faithful fan club watching or listening to Dad on the air than his five children and his wife. At times his comments are amusing and poor Dad is kept humble by us reminding him of his phraseology! He was being interviewed one evening regarding security and the leak of information about a British ambassador's travel plans in Eire which got into the IRA's hands. In closing his reply he said,

'Of course we all have to watch our backsides when it comes to personal security'. We knew what was meant but the picture conjured up was quite different. I wondered also if Dad was

being subtle in his suggestion that most politicians' brains were
in that locality! Speaking of brains and security matters, once
at a rally I listened to an Englishman describe a shooting
attempt on the life of a Northern Ireland councillor. He said,
'The bullet went right through his head and didn't hit
anything vital!' (Actually, knowing the councillor concerned,
I think it was an accurate statement!)

Whether we like it or not, the press are necessary and quite
frankly I do sometimes wonder what their image of *us* must
be. Perhaps the most vital lesson for the public to learn is not
to believe everything it reads. It is just another interpretation
or opinion by a person who, no matter how objectively he
writes, still has a bias one way or the other. Because something
appears in quotes does not mean it is in context. I remember
watching Dad at the conclusion of a pretty rough protest
against the presence of the Secretary of State at a function
after the signing of the Anglo-Irish Agreement; he was being
interviewed for about the sixth time. Dad was in rare form.
The interview turned out to be Dad questioning the poor guy,
a foreigner who was totally out of his depth. He was quite
small in build, and had a cartoonist been on the scene, he would
have had material in abundance for a comic strip. At home
later, when the dust had settled, the funny side of the thing hit
me and I said:

'Dad, you didn't half get stuck into that wee foreign
reporter.'

'I know, he replied, in a serious tone, 'I was thinking about
that wee fellow. The poor critter hadn't a clue what was going
on. His questions were stupid but I was far too sore on him.
I really feel sorry that I said anything.'

That wee fellow will think he has met 'big Ian Paisley' I
thought, but he hasn't at all. Caught in an instant we can all
appear extreme at times. Granted, a man's extreme remarks
make good headlines, but how easily people lose sight of the
human nature behind the profiles created by the media.

There is nothing which I see or read about in the press that
doesn't make me wonder what the other side of the story is.
Contention with other political representatives is unavoidable.

Many not involved in political life seem to think that heated debate is automatically followed through into personal relationships, which of course is not the case. Unfortunately there are some pea-brained would-be politicians around Ulster who do behave like that.

CHAPTER TEN

A Year to Remember

I was trailing the vacuum cleaner down the stairs at home one Saturday morning in the late spring of 1986, when Mum called to tell me there was a 'phone call. It was Sammy Wilson. I have known Sammy for years, having met him as a student while I was still at school. My father and his, both ministers, have been associated for longer than I remember but our paths crossed only occasionally after those early years until, through serving on the local Council, we saw each other more often. Sammy is the DUP group leader in the Council and as I am secretary, there were jobs to be done together. It was the end of my first year as a councillor and Sammy had been a helpful friend. He had just won the DUP group nomination to be our contender for the upcoming position of Lord Mayor, from June 1986 to June 1987.

I went to the 'phone and after talking a few minutes he informed me of the purpose of his call – he was wondering if I would think about being Lady Mayoress if he won the position. We agreed that I'd give him a ring after the weekend – I believe the Council was to be either that Monday or the next.

I must admit I wasn't quite sure if I wanted the job at first. I didn't know what it entailed. I didn't know how it would affect my work and I wondered if Sammy could stick me for a year! On Sunday I mentioned it to Mum and Dad.

'You should do it,' said Dad – 'there no reason why not.' I

thought .– he's right. Work keeps and whatever else it entails, it will be an experience and I ought to have a crack at it. My decision was made. Mum and Dad were happy enough and talking over the immediate concerns I had, made me content that it was the right decision. As it turned out, Sammy did win the vote, and so began a year to remember. Looking back, it wasn't the easiest year I've faced in my life, but it certainly was one of the best. I learnt a double lesson – about conflict and about humour.

We had thoroughly good times and we had thoroughly hard times – times when you could please nobody. I am a different person from the lessons I learnt during the difficulties, and I hope I am different because of the happiness I enjoyed also.

For me the conflicts which were to mark that period were more associated with the fact I was the moderator's daughter than that I was the Party leader's daughter. The politics were easier to handle. 'Belfast Says No' was the theme of our year and the issue was so cut and dried, that to tailor our actions to it turned out to be a simpler task than I'd imagined. I believed in what Sammy was aiming to do, so trying as best as I could to give support was not a hard thing.

What I did not expect was the barrage from disapproving Christians who seemed intent to review everything with a fine tooth comb. I'm afraid by one quarter of the way into the term I was already branded 'backslidden' and in the eyes of those who so judged me, I remain in that status! To them, for a Christian to associate themselves with social functions, with forms of entertainment and so on was totally unacceptable.

At first I was upset. The initial accusations stung. I questioned hard my own aims and apparent testimony and felt somewhat confused. This though, is not a dangerous nor detrimental thing to do, for you learn just how much you are prepared to take from others, and how much your personal beliefs really mean. The twist to the argument which I found most perplexing and difficult to overcome was when the accuser referred to the effect that my views or actions were having on Dad's ministry. What generally happened was, that when the accuser of the moment saw that I wasn't about to change to fit their particular image of my role, they twisted the knife by telling me that I was 'ruining' all Dad stood for.

It sickened and angered me that an outsider could dare to step over the line and try to damage the relationship between a father and a daughter. There were no arguments between me and Dad. I was not hurting him or his ministry, but it can be daunting enough trying to convince yourself of this in the middle of a fray. I remember one early instance in particular. It had been a week of one thing on top of another. My youth work had been disastrous, things were heated on the political front and it was proving to be a hectic week at City Hall as well. Then, of course, just to ice it, there had to be somebody 'concerned about my spiritual well-being'! I listened, but really didn't have the time to react as I was driving off to some function. I knew I would have to tell Dad because they were intent on seeing him about the matter. It is at such times you realise how adamant the Devil is.

I hadn't intended coming in for tea due to the amount of work I had, but I knew it would be the only time I'd have a chance to see Dad. He was watching the news, having had something to eat, and the police car was already waiting to take him to a meeting. I went into the room and said:

'Dad, can I have a word?'

'Yes, what is it? Put the TV off, there's nothing else on that I want to watch anyway.'

'This morning . . .' I began, and as much to my own surprise as Dad's, I burst into tears.

My father simply never permits anything to interfere when we need him. He let me settle down and then we talked – taking time as though he had the whole night and there was no car waiting. He knew it was important that we talked before the other party approached him, otherwise their interpretation would more than likely be that I didn't communicate with Dad! It wasn't solved overnight, and many other frictions arose as a result, but I was learning – and no one ever had me in tears again.

In fact with Dad and me it became 'Here we go again' or 'Well, what is it this time?' Usually, of course, it is me sympathizing with my father, since he is the one who gets most of the criticism. Sometimes I get nauseated at people's harsh judgment of him – people whom he has helped, employed, encouraged and done right by – yet they are the first to respond negatively if they hear a compliment paid to him. Such people are plain 'users' and someday my charity towards them will, I fear, no longer prevent me exploding all over them!

The criticisms were bound to come. Life is like that. It is best to meet them with caution, trying to discern the constructive from the destructive, reacting to each according to their merit. But it is necessary not to let other people's opinions become your guide, otherwise you turn yourself into a pawn. People don't like you to assert yourself.

The fact is that there is a cultural trend in Ulster which I doubt will ever be altered. Here, if you do not agree with someone who has a very rigid and impossibly traditional view, you aren't just wrong, you are a traitor! You aren't just of a different opinion, you are an apostate. Tolerance and forgiveness have been hijacked by insipid clergy and willowy politicians. Tolerance is only tolerance when you can hold an opinion or a belief strongly yet accept the other's right to differ as strongly. It is no test or evidence of tolerance to accept someone's view when you are apathetic or have no strong opinion. Therefore true tolerance has no need to avoid truth. Forgiveness is something which ultimately only God can instigate. We may have the ability – more often due to His grace in us – to have a forgiving spirit towards those who have wronged us, but forgiveness can only be granted when repentance is evidenced. The world has hailed and been inspired by the forgiving attitude of many who have suffered unjustly, not only in Ulster. Those Christians, for example, behind the Iron Curtain, who, after horrific mental and spiritual torture, have survived to relate their experiences, present a rare insight into the power of God in an individual life.

My memories of the year are stronger in their joy than in their dismay. It was a lively and pleasant job to do. Sammy was easy to get along with and his capable, natural way with people was a tremendous asset. He was a credible, young politician at the start of the year and by its conclusion, that credibility had won him respect and, I believe, the hearts of those he sought to work for.

There were enemies made – there were converts made – but there was a job well done by him which raised not just his own profile but that of the party and, of immediate importance, that of the Joint Unionist protest against the Anglo-Irish Agreement. The previous year had seen John Carson as Lord Mayor. His concern appeared to rest more upon his popularity and desire for knighthood than upon the urgency of seeing the Agreement dealt with. Sammy's stand was like a breath of fresh air for the majority whose will was being ignored.

There are two speeches which Sammy made that remain outstanding in my mind. One was at the second 'Ulster says No' rally at the City Hall in November 1986. It came across as a very fervent, determined speech but it was propelled into active force by the sheer atmosphere and appeal of the crowds. I don't recall it getting much cover in the press, in fact, nor did the two leaders' speeches because of the orchestrated trouble which broke out among about forty at a nearby corner to the platform.

The other was at a much smaller occasion. The opening of an extension hall to a mission work on the Shankhill Road. The purpose of the hall was to help the unemployed and those in need. His remarks that day were from a believer's point of view and were warm but practical – an aspect of Christianity which I wholeheartedly agree with. The spiritual isn't coddled in some unearthly blanket. It is the outworking of faith that most tells in this world and these sentiments were expressed with as much determination and fervour – albeit in a necessarily quieter style – as were the sentiments expressed politically. I'm glad Christianity isn't all Amens, Hallelujahs and staid meetings. Had Wilson's brand been so, I know I'd never have made it through a year's work with him!

Sammy was like a big live toy for Dad! He had any visitor to Ulster arranged to meet 'the first DUP Lord Mayor'. I don't think that the Lord Mayor's rooms ever were host to such a diverse conglomeration of activities before. There was such a sense of liveliness to the year, the protests, the informality, our constant flow of young friends, all made the marble of the City Hall reflect that there was a new generation around not tied to gold brocade and ostentatious cars.

Around June 1986, we weren't too long into things when the outgoing Lord Mayor's secretary summoned us. She was very diplomatic in her approach and had spoken with Sammy first before coming into my room.

'Lady Mayoress,' (the staff always called you by the title), 'Lady Mayoress, what I have to tell you is of utmost confidentiality and even your nearest and dearest must not know.' I wondered if someone had Aids. 'There is to be a royal visit tomorrow.'

'Flip me!' I thought. 'I've never been into royalty.'

'Now here is the agenda. I have a telephone call to make,' she continued, looking at her watch, 'so I'll leave it with you and will be back in a moment should you have any questions.' The names of the visitors were Tipp-exed out so I shuffled through the papers, read the details and then held them to the light to get the names. The secretary returned.

'Well, is there any difficulty with the times?' We have cleared any other engagements in the diary so there will be no problems.'

'Everything's fine,' I said, and wanted to laugh. I gave her my word not to mention it and she left. I dandered into Sammy's office.

'Royal visitors – what a privilege!' I said. He was no more taken with the idea than me.

'Fergie and Andy,' he replied.

'Did you hold the papers up to the light too?' I said, and we both really laughed. Honestly, the whole thing was daft – such an infantile way to treat Ulster citizens. The Royal Family are being used by successive British governments in Ulster as a sop to the Loyalist community. They are flown over and helicoptered around at periodic times when convenient politically. Should an 'Enniskillen' occur, they are the perfect consolation. Ulster has had too many Enniskillens that have been chosen to be ignored by British governments, so they are only misleading themselves if they think Ulster Loyalists fall for their royal stage acts. I hope the Royal Family sees through it.

My family were always keen to know how things were getting along and we used to have some hilarious times telling them about the functions of the day or week, depending how long it was between our little family gatherings. One evening we had a celebration to attend in the famed Welders' Club of the Shipyard. We were there a little after its opening due to another duty and upon our arrival there were some attenders already well oiled. We were taken to our seats and I was placed between two ladies. One was tipsy, the other happy! Sammy was a couple of seats down from me and had been nabbed by Roy Bradford who writes for the Belfast Newsletter. They were deep in debate about politics so mine was the task of conversing with the two women.

'Well, love,' began the one on my left, 'have you an' him (nodding at Sammy) any children yet?'

'No,' I said, unable to contain a huge smile.

'Och,' said she before I could explain anything, 'sure, you's are both young, there's plenty of time yet – are you's wanting children?'

'No,' I said still grinning.

'Oh, I see,' she said, somewhat taken aback through her tipsyness. 'How long are you married? Is that it? Are you's just married?'

'We aren't married,' I replied.

'Oh, I see,' she said, her eyes a little larger now. 'Well, I suppose you's will be married once you get this year over you?'

'No, we aren't planning to get married,' I said.

'Oh, I see,' came the slow reply, along with a distasteful look.

'Sammy already is married,' I continued.

'Oh, I see,' she said, now looking at me in complete disgust. I was still smiling and no doubt that fact alone made her think me the more brazen. Her friend had desperately been trying to get her attention throughout this conversation but she had waded on in, determined not to be deterred in her pursuit of gossip and, I admit, I sat back and let her! A few minutes later she nudged me.

'Dear, I'm awfully sorry, I really am – I wasn't meaning to infer anything you know. I understand your position now. I'm awful sorry.'

'That's OK,' I said . . . yes, still smiling! Trying to redeem herself she went on,

'So what do you do?' I told her.

'And whereabouts in Belfast do you live?' I told her.

'What does your father do?'

'He's a minister.'

'Oh, where?'

'His church is on the Ravenhill Road.'

'Is it – would it be near where Paisley's is?'

'It is Paisley's,' I said with a giggle. The poor soul – she was sober instantly. After a stare and a good minute's pause she said,

'Oh my word, I know who you's are now! My goodness, and I've been saying all these things. Oh, love I'm sorry, I really am.'

'Never mind,' I said. 'I didn't think anything of it.' Thankfully it was time to do our social duty and start mixing among the people, moving from table to table, but what a laugh we had about that night afterwards!

No doubt the fact that Sammy and I weren't married caused confusion for many who presumed the Lady Mayoress was always the Lord Mayor's wife. One wee boy, once he knew we weren't married, said to Sammy,

'Well then, if you're the Lord Mayor, is she the Lord Woman?'

The staff we had around us were a great group to work with. I wondered how they survived us sometimes with our protests, parties and jokes. At Christmas we had Rod Hull, the ventriloquist, in Belfast as the city's guest for the switching on the Christmas lights. He had a rousing welcome and somebody sent Sammy a little Emu toy as a keepsake. To be honest, we were sick to death of Emu after a while so one night I had remained to do some written work after everyone was gone. Cherith called to give me a lift home well after midnight, and we were in a humourous mood. Cherith spied the bird and said,

'Whose is that thing?' I explained and concluded by saying, 'I'd love to hang it from that chandelier!'

'Let's!' we chorused. So there I was at 2 a.m. on top of a table in the Lord Mayor's study being handed string and a puppet bird to hang. We attached a suitable suicide note and left. Everybody that came into the room the next morning jumped in shock so we left him there for the day just to watch everyone's reaction. It ranged from,

'What the – !' to

'My word!' to

'Arggh!' Then we ceremoniously took down his remains and laid them to rest.

Another function at the City Hall ended very late and had been a tedious affair. We had returned to the private rooms to get a drink and let the place clear before we left. At times when functions are on, the corridors leading to the Lord Mayor's rooms are roped off. The place was deserted when we were leaving but the cordon was still in place. Three members of staff were leaving with us and Sammy and I suggested we have a wee skip using the leather covered rope. It took a moment's persuasion but they obliged and turned the rope for us. Talk about getting nostalgic! They were harder to stop than us, for they began chanting all the skipping tunes from their childhood days! We initially only knew a couple, but by half-an-hour's time our repertoire was greatly increased. The festivities came to an abrupt end when during one of the fast competitions Sammy tripped on the rope, fell over and ripped his trousers.

'Right, children!' said the driver, who knew when to inject sanity into our tomfoolery. 'That's enough. I don't want to have to drive you home via casualty.'

There were groups of every shape, size and form to receive. During one of these group visits a tour was arranged, as was common practice at the City Hall. When it was a more private affair and a small number it was possible to get included in the tour a walk to the top of the dome. On one such occasion I accompanied some visitors up the dome for on a clear night it is a beautiful view over the city. There were only about six or seven of us who had chosen to go up – three of whom were public speakers. One of these remarked,

'I wonder how far our voices would carry from here?' After some debate as to how far and the way a voice would carry, we decided to experiment. It was quite late but there were still several people in the streets below, so we decided to give a shout simultaneously and see if we got a reaction.

'What will we shout?' said one.

'Belfast says no,' I suggested. We laughed and –

'One, two, three . . . Belfast says no!' They heard but nobody knew where it was coming from. Again:

'Belfast says no!' It was getting funnier. Two policemen on duty below were baffled. Again:

'Belfast says no!' The poor guide was doing his nut.

'I'm away,' he said and took off. Laughing, we followed him and as we came to the bottom of the spiral stairway we were met by at least a dozen policemen tearing up the huge marble staircase. Their colleagues had radioed that an illegal protest was going on and of course they had to come running. Our amusement was increased – theirs was non-existent. Needless to say, ask as I might, I never did get to take a bunch of friends out onto the dome again.

The chains of office belonging to Belfast are beautifully crafted pieces of work. The Lady Mayoress' chain has many precious stones, intricate gold work and fine enamelling. It has a matching bracelet which I only wore on rare occasions as it was quite large and easily slipped off my hand, and I wore it only if I had on a short-sleeved dress so that I could keep an eye on it.

It was my father's fortieth anniversary as minister of our church and a dinner was being held in his honour. We had been invited as official guests. I had the bracelet on and during an interval in the proceedings went to the loo. As I closed the cubicle door and turned around, the bracelet slipped lightheartedly off my wrist and straight down the toilet. There I was having to rescue the precious thing, my arm half-way down 'the bog'. (Had I already gone, the thing, precious or not, would have remained in its watery grave!) I went back to the sink and proceeded to give it and my arm a thoroughly good wash, much to the amazement of those women waiting their turn. They must have thought me hyper about cleanliness! Imagine the scene:

'Well, Town Clerk, it's like this . . .' Worse still – imagine the Sunday papers!

The humour associated with Council has by no means limited to that year. As an elected representative I have found that constituency calls many times lead to amusing situations. One of the funniest that I have heard was an incident that occurred to Sammy. The husband could only hear if you shouted directly into his ear and the wife was blind. Both were aged. Sammy had to call on this particular couple about their case and when the man came to the door, the following took place:

'Oh Mr Wilson, I'm awfully glad to see you. I've lost my wife.'

'Och dear, I'm very sorry to hear that,' shouted Sammy in his ear. When did it happen.'

'Just about two hours ago.'

'My goodness! What happened.'

'She just went up the stairs, and I haven't seen her since.'

Only then did the penny drop and the dull hammering in the background make sense! She wasn't 'lost' in the sense Sammy had imagined, but lost literally. So Sammy had to take off up stairs and search the rooms to find the blind woman frantically hammering from inside a wardrobe whose door she had mistaken for the hallway door! He couldn't get out of the place quick enough to have a good laugh!

Our year working together passed quickly. It was busy and seemed to get busier as the months went on. One of the nicest evenings we spent was at its conclusion when we enjoyed a meal out with the staff as a totally private dinner. It was lovely to share their company in a non-working relationship and away from the City Hall. The people whose lives cross paths with our own ought always to be worthy of time.

I remain indebted to Sammy for asking me to work alongside him that year. It was beneficial to me to learn from his method of working and from his political tactics. I don't know that we would agree on everything but we never had occasion to fall out! I am glad of his influence from a personal point of view also and I respect him greatly for his own personal testimony as a child of God. He became a dear friend with whom I count it a privilege to be associated.

At the beginning of that year Dad said to me as we walked downstairs at home,

'It won't be easy, but whatever you do – set your mind to enjoy it.'

'I will,' I said. For some reason his words never left me and his advice, as always, proved sound, practical and right. It carried me through the harder patches and it added depth to the lighter times. Doing a job 'with simplicity . . . with diligence . . . and with cheerfulness,' as Romans 12:8 suggests, is the best method anyone can have for their work, no matter what it is.

CHAPTER ELEVEN

Evangelism

The word 'evangelist' has always conjured up in my mind an extremely active picture. It suggests urgency and power, yet the 'evangel' sound in it implies tenderness.

When Dad is asked his occupation he always replies, 'Minister of the Gospel'. Whatever else Dad does he is always first a preacher. I don't like that description of Dad – it has much too distorted an image. Nowadays, 'Preach it!' is the mouth cry of blinkered legalists. Anyone I've heard shout 'Preach it, brother!' in a meeting does nothing but sit home and condemn every other active Christian. It is only a cry from the teeth out, because the heart is already decomposed.

I think of Dad always as an evangelist. His ministry is not limited to his pastorate. He travels the world to proclaim Christ, and his care, his regard for those in need, his ingenuous handling of God's Word and his power of oratory, make him an evangel. It would be a very easy thing for my father, now in his sixties, to fall into a comfortable style of evangelism just as it is easy for a painter to produce a certain style of a picture just because there is a market for it. There is a certain safety with the familiar, but this safety is the greatest barrier against any type of development – whether it be intellectual, artistic, political or evangelistic.

In fundamentalist circles, it is hard to win approval for any new venture. That is the aspect of Dad's life's work which I most appreciate. He never hesitated to be radical when it came to reaching those in need. As a young minister, he opened his little church building on a Friday night to have a place to bring drunks in, to sober them up, to give them soup, and to show in a practical way Christ's love for them. It was disapproved of and some forty years ago it must have been traumatic for church members to accept, because I know many a church today that still would not permit such a use of their 'sanctuary'. What irony! What use is a sanctuary if it cannot be opened to give refuge? But at those Friday night meetings many a man found Christ, and his life was reformed. Our church is the richer for their contribution, for it is a very true fact that whoever is forgiven most, loves the most.

As youngsters, before Dad's political involvement began, we often accompanied him at weekends to whatever mission he was engaged in. The Free Presbyterian Church at that time did not have many established congregations, and so Dad's missions were usually held in tents. The mission resulted in the formation of a church work in that area. Always many accepted Christ as Saviour.

We are saved by grace, through faith *unto works*. If our lives, no matter what our occupation may be, do not evidence Christ, our faith is a corpse and God's grace is its coffin instead of the catalyst it is engineered to be. Perhaps the greatest problem in personal evangelism is that we are just not ourselves. The key in communicating Christ surely is obedience, not a doctorate in theology. Being who you are as an individual is important and necessary. God does not redeem us to clone us. Of course we don't have all the answers – so what? Does a mathematician or a politician? To let ourselves be prevented from sharing the friendship we have with Christ is the greatest admission of pride we signal to the world – we won't or don't mention Christ in case we look stupid! I'd rather look stupid if that's what I'm condemned as, than watch my friends, my work colleagues and anyone else my life touches, face a lost eternity because I chose to let my bashfulness be good enough to excuse my responsibility.

The whole theme of evangelism and personal witness is one which the individual cannot ignore once Christ has become their Lord. There are many around us who never will be touched by any traditional evangelistic medium. This is something which has been part of my upbringing, since evangelism is a way of life for both my parents. The challenge of trying to relate the offer of salvation in some way to hundreds of unchurched young people has in turn involved me in voluntary youth work. After only a few months doing outreach among teenagers who were living away from home and in some cases homeless, who had got involved in drug abuse and had problems related to drink, it was blatantly clear to me how much need there was in this area. The voluntary project became my full-time occupation, now under the sponsorship of our Church. We have since opened a drop-in centre as a base for this work close to the city centre.

If evangelism is to succeed in penetrating the whole world, you must use every rightful method at your disposal. When Paul said in his first letter to the Corinthians 'I am made all things to all men, that I might by all means save some' (9:22), surely what he was urging upon us is flexibility, not duplicity. Today evangelism faces constant temptations to use impersonal techniques as a substitute for the costly involvement of personal friendship and concern – costly because it does demand time, energy, patience, compassion, love – often with frugal results for many months and with more criticism than encouragement from others! A major obstacle is narrowness of approach which fails to take advantage of *every* means God has placed at our disposal. Refusal to change methods is as great a danger to evangelism as any attempt to change the message. Preserving and improving old techniques ought to be done but we need to be as eagerly creative and imaginative when trying new forms of evangelism. We cannot justify our lack of willingness with the excuse that the old methods worked before and to update is 'compromise' with the world. What utter hypocrisy can seep through our stony hearts to assuage the Holy Spirit's promptings to go the second mile in order to present Christ to those who so desperately need him! Too many Christians follow the example of a Christless society in condemning the young girl who becomes pregnant outside marriage instead of pouring into her life the healing oil of the Master's care and remembering with a contrite heart that it could easily have been their own daughter, had it not been for the grace of God. Too many despise the young man who pumps his veins full of whatever dope his fumbling hands can grasp and view his pathetic dependent life as the result of a weak character instead of remembering that his soul is as precious to God as theirs and the same blood atones. The 'elder brother spirit' is the most detrimental that a Christian can employ because it leaves condemned the sinner and it leaves disheartened and discouraged the soul-winner.

Evangelism is the warm, spontaneous and human effort of communicating Christ so that the Holy Spirit is given all the glory when by his grace the evangel reaches and, when that same grace mingled with mercy, convicts and wins. We must interest people in the fact that belief in God and Christ's work of atonement *can* make a difference to their daily lives. In the New Testament witnessing covered a spectrum of approaches – to say flexibility and imagination are not in keeping is to drop from our armoury a vast wealth of weaponry.

In youth work today it is vital that we bring the message of salvation to this generation in the authority of the scriptures, yes – but also that we link it to the realities of unemployment, leisure, illness and every other influence of the world. But even in such a tender, important and urgent aspect of our lives, others are interfering. I use the word interfere in the sense of meddling, because it is a prying that is uncalled for. Galatians 6:4 says,

'Let every man prove his own work and then he shall have rejoicing in himself and not in another.' The chapter goes on to say, 'As we have opportunity let us do good unto all men, especially unto them who are of the household of faith.' In following the pattern, Christ has outlined for us in the scriptures we are to do it 'that we should be to the praise of his glory'. To fulfil this we must be happy in our work and activities – we cannot be happy if those of the 'household of faith' set themselves to pour ice over us! It is not that I am blind to advice, but I have learnt (and in a hard enough school) to follow what I believe, to make my own way, otherwise the various directions demanded by the dictates of disconcerted, self-righteous, legalistic 'Christians' would long since have driven me and my family to distraction! There is no law against the fruits of the Spirit which are 'love, joy, peace, longsuffering, gentleness, goodness, faith, meekness, temperance' (Galatians 5:22). We are each better employed to take these and practise them than to take on the role of a judge.

How far overlooked the mercy of Christ is, how distant the Christ who wept over Jerusalem is placed, how remote the hand that inspired the words, 'If any man thirst let him come to me and drink.' Such aches can be met only by Christ and yet his body on earth is often responsible for proclaiming these astounding claims of Christ with their lips while denying them by their lifestyle. The total depravity of man surely is no more clearly depicted when one sees this eagerness to pass judgement on others and the slowness with which mercy ploughs. What a contrast to Jesus Christ who is slow in wrath and swift in mercy! Christianity today is described as being 'watered down' in its message. The case often is not that it has been watered down, but that the flow of Christ's spirit has been prevented and the water that can satisfy has been let form a pool which stagnates and flows nowhere.

It would be very hard to decide which is the worst – watered down, ecumenical Christianity which mixes with everything so much its identity is lost, or jelled Fundamentalism which is too solid to permit entrance of anything more fluid in to its body.

In the work in which I am involved, quick conversions are the exception, not the norm. The majority of our contacts are caught up in drug abuse; drink problems are common, as are unwanted pregnancies. The majority have never been churchgoers. To expect a youth to change appearance, lifestyle, habits overnight is unrealistic. Granted, it can and has happened but there is no evidence that it is what should always occur. While people would not tolerate many of the 'sins' of some contacts, they do tolerate and would even explain away other acceptable sins in the church. As far as I understand, such things as gossiping, temper and gluttony are sin according to scripture. It's rare that these are viewed on a par with such things as drunkenness or drug addiction. I've yet to hear those who are valium addicts among believers be faced with the fact they depend more upon their valium bottle than upon the promises of God's word. 'All unrighteousness is sin,' so there is no-one who ought to have the audacity to point the finger until they have had a good honest look at themselves. We have high expectations of a poor dope addict or an alcoholic who has never known the way of salvation whilst we place almost no expectation upon the church gossips and bad tempered members who have been raised all their lives in the pew. Try reaching the lost and soon you learn how petty-minded Christianity can let Satan drag it. What most appealed to me about Jesus Christ was that he accepted me just as I was and still he accepts me as I am. There are no prerequisites. I didn't have to do anything, I had no holy order of works to attain and no pious spirituality to create – I came as I was and then his Spirit did the alteration. Still, as his purchased child by Calvary's finished atonement, he takes me for what I am and loves me. He has often to chastise me for I am by no means a saint, but he never distances himself. If there is any distancing done, it is a result of my rebelliousness or waywardness, not lack of care from him. There is nothing greater than the friend-ship of Christ for anyone to have in life and death. He doesn't change. He doesn't fail. These eternal truths have been imparted to me by the evangelism of my father's life. I don't hit the same pace as he does. I have a different approach to many things than he does, but Christ only asks for our personal best, not to keep up with John the Baptist, Paul the Apostle or Ian Paisley. In Jesus we have not only a Saviour, but a dear, dear friend. This is what makes faith bright and puts laughter in it. His words are, as the psalmist puts it, 'comfortable'; they fit perfectly. He is 'the altogether lovely one'.

In personal witnessing Dad never abruptly corners anyone. He steers the conversation via the person's interests on to Christ. Yes, he seeks for opportunities to do so and having first prayed that he will see and grasp such opportunities, God

has and continues to give him as fruitful a ministry in personal
evangelism as in his public pulpit ministry. Jesus Christ spent
more of his earthly ministry with individuals than he did
proclaiming to multitudes. Why is this pattern not good
enough for the vast majority of Christians today?

Dad's evangelism is a demanding business. He is not a cleric
who reads polite little prayers about flimsy poetic injustices nor
is he a parson who has wee theses which he stands up and
reads in a ministerial voice. His ministry has prayer as its first
priority. I have never known anyone to emphasise prayer as
strongly as Dad, and in a personal way before a public way.
Now, he doesn't pray and sit down and do nothing. He prays
and gets at the job. To pray and do nothing is as daft as sitting
down with a sketch pad and expecting the scene before you to
appear on paper without lifting the pencil to draw it. This is
one of the most valuable things Dad has passed on to us, his
children – even though family worship was not always easy!
During one summer holiday, two of my cousins were staying
with us. The male one was quite young at the time and not
used to our system of working, so when he realised that he
was going to have to pray 'out loud' he simply couldn't cope
and dissolved into sobs which became audible as he was asked
to pray.

'What's wrong, dear?' asked Mum.

'I don't want to pray out loud!' he sobbed pitifully. The rest
of us, including his sister, were totally unsympathetic and all
sat looking out between our fingers at each other, sniggering.

'Of course you won't have to pray,' said Dad, lifting him
onto his knee to console him.

'Huh!' thought the rest of us, 'wish we'd tried that one!'

Despite the trials of attempting to read scripture aloud (in
the King James' Version, of course), we all survived and in fact
the words often stumbled over by our young mouths wove
their way throughout our daily lives to become meaningful to
us and to become loved by us. Family worship continues to
have its amusing moments, but it remains an important aspect
of home life for us still which keeps us unified in many ways.
While our individual responsibilities and work steer us in

various directions, family worship rectifies the balance and redresses our attention to each other when it would be easy to take that bond for granted.

Prayer is for everyone and it is our direct link with Jesus Christ. It is not some formalised communication that must be ornately worded and grammatically precise. It is simply talking with him as a dear, close and precious friend. I would have given up any pretence of Christianity long ago if I didn't believe in this type of individual, personal and loving relationship with Jesus Christ. Dad's vitality as a minister stems from this happy and hopeful friendship with Christ – he died for the individual. My father is Calvinistic but he is not hyper. Salvation is a gift extended to all and he presents the gospel to anyone who will listen.

I read a story once about a young preacher who was hung up on predestination. He asked an older minister,

'How will I know if I have converted the right person?' To which the wise old man answered,

'Laddie, don't worry. I'm sure God will forgive you if you get the wrong one.'

To get caught up on any one issue is a very foolish thing. Being a minister's child means that you are faced with everyone's wee pet doctrine. How a believer can waste time pontificating over earrings or make-up, the millenium and the rapture, if Moses had blue eyes or John had a beard – I mean, what does it matter? There's a whole world of need now. One of the pleasing aspects of my work has been to have opportunity to take contacts, both Protestant and Roman Catholic alike, to meet Dad. He gives them time, listens to them, and their questions he patiently answers. It is too bad the world media show a positive distaste for this aspect of my father's nature and the few who have seen it treat it as a PR exercise. Sarcasm is the hallmark of their comments. Evangelism has made Dad long suffering. That is why he can keep going. He doesn't measure his life by what he can get but by what he can give. Therefore he has more to contribute to this age than most. His strength stands in his loss – loss of selfishness. Many times I have seen Dad absolutely tired out, yet he goes on. To be honest, I have often used my tiredness as an excuse not to do anything. He doesn't, and so his tiredness becomes a witness. I recall this thought striking me not that long ago. We were attending a service as a family with Dad. It was during an Opening Mission in our Hillsborough church. What a fortnight it had been and that day in particular was extremely hectic for him. As a family we knew he was tired and to top it all, he had a miserable cold. Yet there he was, as willing, as astute, as brilliant as though he'd just enjoyed a week's holiday. To me that was one of the finest witnesses a man could evidence to a people and the very weakness of humanity was taken and used to proclaim Christ. I thought how, when physically tired, Jesus didn't use that as an excuse not to uplift his Father but as the very pivotal point of his testimony to the woman of Samaria. Surely the most impact we can have as believers is to walk alongside this world, not aloof from it. Using the everyday experiences we have as a means of presenting Christ.

There was one occasion, some years ago now, that Dad couldn't make it to a mission. He was really sick with a 'flu bug which was successfully doing the round of our house. Mum also had it. The student who had gone along to preach for him by way of apology said,

'I know many of those who are here tonight came especially to hear Dr Paisley. Well, I'm sorry that he is not here – he is in bed with his wife!'

As a result of the youth work, sometimes contacts accepted the invitation to attend a church service. Some are punk in their styles of dress and living. Two guys were with me one Sunday evening and the way we had walked into the pew meant that I was sitting between them. Often their concentration wanes, not being accustomed to church attendance and this particular evening nothing seemed to grasp their attention. They shuffled about, they whispered across to one another and at last one of them quietened, having found something in his studded leather jacket which obviously amused him. He futered with this thing and moved it around. He handed it across to his mate, who in due course handed it back. All the while I was trying to ignore the activity. Dad was nearing the conclusion of his message and quoted these words by Lord Byron:

'My days are in the yellow leaf, the flowers, the fruits of life have gone, the worm, the canker and the grief, are mine alone.' The two perked up instantly upon the mention of the word 'worm' and one leaned in front of me and hung the object of their entertainment on the back of the pew in front. It was a long, half squashed, dead worm!

At the conclusion of another service to which two other contacts had come, we had arranged to meet with Dad afterwards to discuss an urgent matter regarding their situation. They were living together and the girl had become pregnant. She wanted to have an abortion but the boy who had been raised in a devout Roman Catholic home was not so certain. Dad had agreed to their request to talk things over. It was a heavy conversation and the pair were obviously at odds over the decision. The girl concerned was very immature in many ways and quite blasé about the whole thing – even frivolous. In the middle of this conversation on such a serious matter, she pulled from her pocket a little fluffy toy and said to Dad,

'Say hello to the bird.'

I couldn't believe it! Dad just looked and said 'hello' and continued the sentence he had been in the middle of. The instant response to her flippancy thankfully worked and she settled down, enabling some progress to be made at last.

When I think that for over forty years Dad has been minister in our church, I find it hard to take in! The size of the harvest he has brought in will only be revealed in eternity.

Evangelism is a way of life for Dad, not just a part of life. Mum's ability as his wife to balance her involvement in his missions with her duties at home have enabled him to fulfil his calling to the vast extent that he has. In evangelism God hasn't meant us all to be in the pulpit – he has meant us to obey in our daily lives. The development of the Free Presbyterian Church is due to the fact Dad has walked the path God desired – accepting its griefs, its burdens and its responsibilities as willingly as its joys – in all things giving thanks.

A negro woman from America once visited Ulster to sing

throughout the province. She was a Gospel singer and had a beautiful talent in her voice. One of my favourite pieces which she sang included these verses:

> The path that I have trod has brought me nearer God,
> Though oft it led through sorrow's gate.
> Though not my way I choose; In my way I might lose
> The joy that yet for me awaits.
>
> Not where I wish to be,
> Nor where I wish to go,
> For who am I that I should
> Choose my way? The Lord shall choose
> For me, 'tis better far I know,
> So let him bid me go or stay.
>
> The cross that I must bear,
> If I a crown would wear,
> Is not the cross that I should take,
> But since on me 'tis laid,
> I'll take it unafraid
> And bear it for the Master's sake.

These verses are a fair summary of the evangel. They express precisely what I have attempted to say about Dad as an evangelist.

CHAPTER TWELVE

Books, Clocks and Gravestones

Years come and go like a child's whisper in the air. Time is short yet mankind is intent to spend what there is of it on secondary things – work before home, self before others, religion before Christ. Materialism and ambition motivate – forcing people to keep pace no matter the cost. More times than not it is loss or defeat that causes us to remember time is short – and many times it is remembered too late. No one can claim discrimination when it comes to time – twenty-four hours of a day is the same duration for everyone. Good use of time is possibly the greatest challenge any of us will ever face, and its outcome is the kindest legacy we can provide for those we care about. Time used constructively means that work is a pleasure, and leisure time is the refreshing space it is purposed to be.

Time is something we have always been acutely aware of in our home. Mum and Dad insisted on certain commitments to ensure this responsibility was taught to us. If any of us fail in maintaining a proper respect for time, it will be through no fault of our parents. In this, as in everything else they sought to instil into our lives, they taught as much by example as by word. Time with and time for one another was a commitment we had to meet. If one of us needed help we were taught to give it willingly even if it meant changing a few things around. 'Charity begins at home'. How sickening it is to see people who are sweet and plausible to everyone bar their own family!

Not only were we taught this commitment to each other, but we also had a commitment to the family as a unit. It was rare when we were young, as it is now, for Dad to have a free evening or day, but if he did we altered our plans to be together. Usually it was at short notice and unless it was an unreasonable change to make, we did so and learnt to do so with a smile.

Many people I have come across are incredibly averse to change. One acquaintance was the sort who, if his mother gave him tomato soup instead of vegetable soup on a Tuesday, his system would not get over it for a month. One day in our house would render him totally useless for a decade. Inability to move with the current, to enjoy its twists and falls, is what I most dread developing. Wanting to stay where you are in age, emotions, in work, would take from me the essence of life with a capital 'L'. Static people are passionless. They have no fervency, the sheer heck of a thing is outrageous to them, even sinful. They remind me of an artificial plant – a green plastic ivy, mass produced in hard plastic soil – unable to grow and good for nothing except collecting dust.

'Godliness with contentment is great gain' should be our goal. Godliness means circulating in the world – not just getting stuck in it somewhere. It means movement, commitment, alertness, involvement, and all that means *change*. How can the child of God become more Christ-like if he becomes stubborn over change?

The most blatant way Dad has made us aware of time is through his clocks, although to be honest I don't think there was any intention in this. He is by no means a serious collector of clocks, but he does like them and has a number of clocks and watches, most of which have been gifts. Every so often, when he has an evening to himself, he takes the urge to get them all wound, reset and ticking. For about a week our house sounds like the shipyard at lunchtime. Chimes and dongs and whirrs and tocks. It would drive you cuckoo (to coin a phrase), if you didn't see the funny side and know that they would run down by the end of the week to let peace reign again for another six months.

One of the times this usually happens is around Christmas when Dad has an hour to two free. He inevitably appears some evening, fresh from his study with about ten clock keys in his hand, an oily rag, and wearing a smile like a Cheshire Cat.

'I've got them all going,' he announces, jubilantly. 'Now it's up to you' (looking at whoever is in the room at the time) 'to keep them going, for I'm not around to do it!'

I learnt my lesson on that one, because being the dutiful daughter (for once) I decided to wind them for him. I used the wrong key in the first, jamming the chimes which repeated 'Oranges and Lemons' for an hour; and the second I wound too tightly so that 'time is short' was proved literally if you referred to it for guidance after that . . . and the third clock I never got near!

When I was writing this book one evening, Dad said,

'Well dear, how's the book coming?'

'Och, I don't think I was half wise to do this book!' was my standard reply to this question, and I went on talking with him, answering his questions about my chapter headings, etc. When I read out the heading for this chapter, 'Books, Clocks and Gravestones', he perked up –

'That's good. I must have a wee talk with you on that one about my books.' The conversation was cut short by the telephone ringing, but Dad never forgets something like that and every week or so afterwards he'd say,

'We must set aside an hour to talk about your book, dear.'

Well, Dad's timetable is ridiculous and two or three arrangements had to be altered. I'd stopped asking and I thought he'd decided to forget it, until one afternoon when I was sitting writing and he said,

'Rhonda, we'll have to do that piece about my books.'

'Well, Dad,' I replied, 'you leave for Africa on Monday' (it was Saturday afternoon) 'and I've to post the script off on Friday. You aren't due home until a week or so later – will you have any time?'

'Right,' he announced, and took out his pocket diary. 'Monday at 10.00 sharp after that other meeting at 9.00.' I

agreed to sort my schedule out to suit this timing. Saturday
night came:

'Rhonda, can you make that 10.30 instead of 10.00? Something has come up.'

On Monday morning, 10.30 came – I waited – 11.00 struck
and there was movement in Dad's office – the appointment
was over – my turn! In I went equipped with pencil and pad.

The phone rang – a problem in a factory over the flying of
a Union Jack (Unionist workers at the time were defying the
Flags and Emblems Act, which makes such gestures illegal).
Immediate action was required.

Three more phone calls and forty-five minutes later I had
precisely two sentences from Dad about books. His next
meeting was at 11.50 – my hour had evaporated.

'This is terrible dear. We'll have to meet later.' Out came
the diary again. 'There's nothing I can change today. I'll be
home from four to five o'clock to pack before leaving for the
airport – can you be free?'

'Yes – see you then.'

'I'm sorry love,' he said with a kiss and a pat on the head,
and we both laughed.

At 3.00 pm, I remember well, I had a Council committee
meeting to attend, but I was determined that no matter what
vote was going on I would be home by four. It was a fiery
meeting: our DUP group were fighting IRA Sinn Fein. The
meeting had to be adjourned to let tempers settle. It reconvened
and business was shoved through. The whole thing was a farce
anyway and I had no scruples about using the Unionist
majority on the committee to do things in such a manner.

The meeting ended swiftly and 3.50 pm saw it close. I made
it home in perfect time (don't tell the speed cops!) but two
other people were waiting. 4.30 pm.

'Ronnie, come up to my study now,' came the call. We
talked about the committee, we talked about what a mess the
day had been and at last we talked about books for fifteen solid
minutes this time.

Dad has some 12,000 volumes in his collection and his ability
to put his hand on the one he requires always surprises us!

As long as Dad can recall, he has been enchanted by books. When he was a child, it was the covers and the illustrations which caught his attention. As he said this I smiled and responded.

'Dad, do you realise the influence art has had on you?' His reply was that he quickly became more, and remains more, impressed by scenes painted with words rather than a brush! I would have contended the point, had not time been so precious.

Books, according to Dad, are just like people – 'some good, some bad, some supreme, some mundane, some princes in their own right, some paupers by choice'. In our conversation Dad referred to the book *Sesame and Lilies* by Ruskin and quoted this passage, saying it well summarised the importance of learning to love reading:

> . . . There is a society continually open to us, of people who will talk to us as long as we like, whatever our rank or occupation; talk to us in the best words they can choose, and of the things nearest their hearts. And this society, because it is so numerous and so gentle, and can be kept waiting round us all day long – kings and statesmen lingering patiently, not to grant audience, but to gain it! – in those plainly furnished and narrow ante-rooms, our book-case shelves – we make no account of that company, perhaps never listen to a word they would say, all day long!

As he spoke I couldn't keep up with him;
'Dad, I can't write that fast!'
'Don't worry – I'll give you the book.'
The first book Dad was introduced to by his father after the Bible was John Bunyan's *Pilgrim's Progress*. He has lost track of the number of times he has read that particular book.
'You know, Dad. I've never read that book even once.' His eyes grew like saucers.
'What, never?'
'Never.'
'That's a disgrace. No wonder you behave the way you do.'
We went on to talk about religious reading and Dad

remarked that his ministerial calling led him to the privilege of studying the 'rich lore of the whole Puritan contribution to theology.'

'No wonder you behave the way you do!' I teased, but he was too far into the Puritans to take any notice of my remark.

Dad loves to read – of that there is no doubt. Reading to him would be like holding pearls and diamonds in both hands, for the richness is as vast to his mind. He reads history, biography and speeches – gleans from them and imparts what he can to us, his children. 'The Book of Books' as he often describes God's Word, is what he reads most – and only the *King James Version*! He views its English as 'a pure well of our language, undefiled'. Each year he reads the Bible through, following a plan of reading established by Robert Murray McCheyne, a Scottish preacher.

'It doesn't age with reading – it becomes newer.'

'One of the worst contributions that other media have made is to take people away from the art, the pleasure and the gain of literature.' A call broke into our conversation:

'The car's here, Ian' said Mum. At which point it was time for Dad to put on his coat, return downstairs, gather his cases and leave for Africa.

Not all our reading was channelled towards the spiritual by Mum and Dad. Their own taste is broader than religious books and resulted in ours being so too. Dad, I must admit, can endure much heavier reading material than I ever could. Forever he comes in after raiding another second-hand book store, with something for all of us. Ian gets something on history, Kyle something on theology, Cherith, poetry and me, art. Initially the art books Dad chose dealt with Renaissance art, Early English work or stained glass, but they have since moved to painters whom he hears me mention: Matisse, Gaugin, Van Gogh, Cezanne, etc. One time we were sitting reading and Dad said,

'What book have you there?'

'It's on Paul Gaugin,' I responded.

'Any good?'

'Great.' I looked at his book; it was Thackeray's *Vanity Fair*.
He had been given a set of Thackeray's works.

'You should read some books on art, Dad,' I jested. 'It would
help your preaching.'

'How?' he laughed.

'Make you creative,' I said.

'OK,' he replied, taking it as a challenge. I'll read that one
on Paul whoever he is when you've done.'

Flip me! I thought – trust me to be into Gaugin at the minute
– but I was not going to argue. A couple of days later I had
finished the books so said to Dad,

'Here you are. It's an interesting biography.' And so it was.
Later on that week Dad came in with a pile of files, papers and
my book.

'I don't think much of the lifestyle of Gaugin – where ever
did you pick that book up?' I couldn't help but grin when I
told him,

'You got me it in some second-hand shop!'

'No wonder it was in a second-hand shop,' he replied, quick
as a shot. We both laughed then talked seriously about Paul
Gaugin's life.

Whenever Dad does read about an artist he is always touched
by their sensitivity and by their creative genius, but most of
all he is moved by the fact that so many have become outcasts
– often simply because they were not understood. Dad is a
creative and sensitive person himself and his own humility
when dealing with people who have, as far as society judges,
fallen short, makes him one of the most compassionate men I
have ever met. His response is continually, 'It could have been
me had not God redeemed my life'. I have yet to meet someone
who claimed that Dad acted self-righteously or proudly in his
dealings with them, no matter how low sin had dragged them,
and no matter how wrecked their lives had become.

Along with books and clocks I always associate gravestones
with Dad. No, he's not morbid nor sordid. But he has this
thing about little pilgrimages to graves where 'people of
achievement' have been laid. People of achievement are
martyrs, covenanters, statesmen and writers. Many a holiday

we spent trekking over the moors to be photographed at some covenanter's grave in Scotland. It was always cold and blowy and the ground uneven and difficult to walk over. There were cowpats galore, and the occasional bull to navigate gingerly – all just to look at some weathered, green, moss-covered stone with a railing around it. Dad would make a wee recording for a slide and voice presentation because more often than not whatever study he was compiling or book he was writing dictated the location of our holiday. I do appreciate the sacrifice made for religious freedom and I am thankful for those men and women of the past who died because of their faith. To be perfectly honest, though, I could have done without the history as such times. Give me a beach, the sun and no media – now that's what I call a holiday.

Still, trekking over the moors did us no harm, and many a laugh we had in the doing. I recall one occasion when Dad insisted that we all climb this hill because of its significance in covenanting history. It was a glorious day and we were quite enthusiastic about the prospect – five zealous children. Off we went and began our afternoon's climb. The reality was that it was a gentle hill, but to children it seemed a mountain and this was a grand adventure: maybe by the time we got to the top it would be foggy or dark and we would have to stay the night. As it was, there were no mists to surround us but an abundance of sheep. In my desire to befriend one which to me was particularly endearing, I began to manoeuvre a barbed wire enclosure but got entangled and my arm got cut. The pale scar it left always reminds me of the holidays we spent trailing around the covenanter land! Knowing about the covenanters and seeing graves of people who lost their lives because of their beliefs made the word 'heritage' understandable. Life had value because it had a cost. As an adult, those childhood lessons have developed in me an acknowledgement that freedom is more than just being outside jail. Freedom is an inward compulsion that desires justice for all peoples. It desires food for the hungry. It desires peace for the broken-hearted. It desires love for the unlovely. It cannot be stopped any more easily than the sun can be stopped from rising. Freedom I will defend but I cannot accept that any other cause is worthy of a man's life. No country is worth a man's life. In Ulster, I have, along with everyone else, witnessed homes for ever changed by murder. Usually it is a wife and children who are left. Has any man the right to declare so strongly a love for his country that leaves his wife and children with soil, but without him? Is it right to establish a bond with a woman who bears your children and the then place yourself so that they are left to life and to the land without you? I don't believe such a declaration can ever be justified. To love one's country first is a cruel and unmanly sentiment. Country is not to be our primary love – we are commanded to love God first and our neighbour as ourselves. Neighbourly love keeps country in its proper place. I mourn with my fellow citizens those who have died because of Ulster's trouble. I shall ever owe a debt to them which cannot be repaid. I can do my utmost to express by actions as well as by words my indebtedness but for those who have set out on a road of 'hero-style' proclmation that taunts the enemy and begs to be a target – for those I have in my blood nothing but contempt. There is too much tragedy, too many disappointments and enough battles to be undertaken in the lives of those we love on earth without adding stress and selfish ambition. Being tender-hearted one to another, loving, caring and being honest; these surely are more worthy pursuits to be engaged in. They are harder and more time consuming to achieve – perhaps that is precisely why we shy away from their challenge. There is no greater achievement to aim our lives towards than loving people. Loving that accepts the individual for what he or she is. Loving that out-loves self. Loving that finds pleasure in gleaning from others in order to improve and heal our own deficiencies so that we might pour back into our heritage wine and not silt. I weary of hearing about my heritage from the lips of those whose claim to it lies in the declaration of it as something which is peculiar to them and their aspect or view of belief concerning it. I tire as much from loyalist rhetoric as I do from republican, and with others of my age group, all I want is peace to enjoy this great heritage I'm supposed to have.

I wonder where we will be in another ten years' time.

Whether the same breaking of homes by murder will endure and in its endurance successfully grind to useless pulp the zest of living? Whether this generation is already lost to its hopes, visions and aspirations because submission to what is worn corrodingly through the days of youth in which these directions are rooted? All these I do wonder about and in dull, rainy, winter days, Ulster's grey feels more intense than can be borne. I sicken to read again the newsboards with their bold black typeface 'MAN SHOT' and the red of the bill shrieks through its little wire rack, its defiance like diseased blood on a glass slide beneath a microscope. Admittedly, at times I don't want to hear details, I don't want to listen to the interviewed family, I don't want to watch the funeral, and least of all do I want to hear the futile condemnations of such 'atrocities'. To keep sane, sometimes you must choose ignorance.

In my more positive moods, I am convinced that this generation, given power for a month in Ulster, could set straight a few matters so that they could claim the advantages of life in our province instead of living more years listening to yesterday's aspirations and watching their youth lost, smudged out by the wash of loyalties that mean nothing to us except betrayal.

It is easy to love the past, but in Ulster it is time to choose the future. Time is short in Ulster – it certainly isn't on our side; we can't afford to play on time for such play is shadowy, dark and frightening and the only certain result is that more deaths will occur while the rules are being read.

I and others of my generation are reaching the conclusion that the old hopes for Ulster will never come to anything – neither by the granting of new rights, nor the winning of more elections, nor by the grenade and the pistol. Only a complete reform of habits, involving genuine repentance and sincere commitment to the country, has any chance of breaking this spiral of violence.

Meanwhile, Ulster's gravestones are monuments to the great wrong of the British Government in her dealing with us as much as they are monuments to the wrong of Irish Republicanism's bloody terror. They represent the many hundreds who will have no opportunity to make such a reform. How many more will lose the opportunity in such a tragic way before our habits change? No government can expect not to forfeit their privilege to govern when they prevent such changes taking place.

My political ideal for Ulster is not as part of the Union, but as an independent state (with Dad as its first President!) By that I mean negotiated independence, not some daft military coup by irresponsible thugs who have lined their pockets by racketeering and who find continual warfare tasteful and a means of financial security. The world needs to take heed of the fact that while Ulster Unionists may be British, they are not English! The attempts of would-be peace-makers to merge what they describe as the two cultures of Ulster may as well be used to try and merge the cultures of the northern English with the southern English. They are quite happy to accept the inherent differences there but not in Ulster.

Now let me make it clear – this is *my* ideal, not my father's nor even that of the D.U.P. I realise that while ideals are pleasing to think and reflect on, they are not always possibilities. An independent Ulster such as the one I mention is merely my immature political dream that lets me smile a little at the thought. I, too, must face reality. 'Ulster is British' is not a lip cry from the majority – it is the heart beat of the people. As a democrat, I can accept their wishes and as a member of the D.U.P. and a councillor for that party, I can work to defend that right. It causes me no difficulties. But if ever I saw a way of achieving independence and if it was the will of the majority, of course I would probably contribute what I could.

Meanwhile, I am no political whizz-kid! I have little experience and in spite of what has appeared in newspaper columns, Dad isn't grooming me, nor anyone else in the family, to take over! I hold a deep respect and loyalty to my father's leadership and have no qualms in saying that I will take his direction as leader until he leaves that position because I trust him.

It is one of the most unfortunate things that the ongoing political and terrorist situation in the province prevents much involvement in major issues which the child of God ought to be active in society. While the violence continues, matters such as health, unemployment, education, agriculture and the environment fall into third, fourth and fifth place. Take the nuclear debate, for instance. This is a matter which affects Ulster as much as it affects the rest of Britain. The disgusting approach of the government to Sellafield with its disastrous consequences upon those living in both Ulster and Eire is a matter of great urgency upon which we have no say whatso- ever, and now the proposed air transportation of the material is yet another serious denial of consideration of those living in Ireland. Let them fly the stuff over Chequers at the weekend I say!

Environmental issues are largely ignored by the media due to the vast extent of coverage which must be directed on the terrorist occurrences of the day. But these issues matter and by the time we wait for the situation to permit them to make headlines, legislation will already have been passed or too much destruction will have occurred to remedy the situation. God has given man dominion over the earth and the responsibility to subdue it, to order it, to meet the needs of the people; not to tear it asunder. We have the pleasant duty of passing this world on the next generation as well preserved as we possibly can. To mock environmentalists as crazy, way-out cases is to cast a very careless rebuff on what is as much a command in God's Word as any one of the Ten.

God save Ulster and give us the sense to let go of what has been in order to have life and a land that's true to its people, not to a relic of the past.

A minister friend of ours – now retired – was at church to preach for my father who was away on an evangelistic campaign. As he entered the building he heard two ladies discuss him. 'It's Rev. Menary this morning' one said. 'Who is he?' replied the other. 'You don't know *him*? He's the greatest has been there has been' was the serious response!

CHAPTER THIRTEEN

The Steps of a Good Man

One Saturday morning, I was doing some work in the Linen Hall Library in the centre of Belfast. As a matter of fact, it was some writing for this book. There is a particular desk which I like to use at one of the windows. The view is interesting and besides, the heating pipes run alongside it, which is cosy in the winter. I happened to be looking out when I saw heads turning in the one direction. I leaned over to see what the attraction was: Dad had just stepped out of his car and was the subject of the looks. I laughed to myself at the thought of my own curiosity's answer.

The steps of my father are watched closely, literally as well as metaphorically. That in itself is a curtailing and difficult pressure to live with. He does take it in his stride and copes with the glare of publicity in his own unique manner. I have heard many say,

'When Paisley goes, the D.U.P. will go too.' I don't think that for one moment but his *will* be a hard act to follow. His approach, direction and abilities are unique to him. To ape them would be to dig your own grave. To top the poll in the country-wide European elections with a province so divided as some would try to make out Ulster is, is no mean achievement. The whole gist of Dad's character is that of an Irishman of Ulster stock. His affable, good-humoured, natural relationship with the electorate has secured him not merely an X on their ballot papers, but a place in their hearts.

That Dad's steps as a politician have maintained an orderly and stable path are rooted in the fact that his calling as a Gospel minister is his first love. He said to me over lunch one day as we were discussing a certain matter regarding another politician.

'Dear, the same could easily have happened to me, if I didn't think I would have to stand each Sunday before my own congregation.' We went on to talk about the importance of having priorities right in life, no matter what sphere of work you did. Somehow, though, I believe that politics has the ability to destroy principle in the individual more callously than many professions.

One reason for Dad's falsely belligerent image is that he is not afraid to recognise that contention is the name of the game in both politics and religious matters. We are to contend for our faith. The Christian's lifestyle is not one of inoffensive weakness, it is one of proclamation, and in many ways, it is one of reclaiming what the Church has let slip away. Dad is a defender and a contender for the faith he cherishes. This does not make him a rough man of war, nor an unreasonable man of attack. The greatest contention any Christian knows is not with human beings. It is what Paul describes as a wrestling with principalities and powers, with spiritual wickedness in high places. It is a constant moulding of our natures to do right as opposed to wrong; to be submissive as opposed to wilful, to be Christ-like as opposed to selfish – to be meek. 'Meekness is not weakness'. Dad is a meek man – he is dynamite under control if you like. The control of his life is in God's hands. His goals have fixed his direction and his destiny. Meekness under Christ, I have seen in Dad's life, means strength and ability to be your best. The artist, Van Gogh, wrote:

> It is good to love many things
> For therein lies strength
> And he who loves much performs much
> And what is done in love is well done.

When I first read that statement Dad came to my mind and

since then I have always associated that quotation with him. When I think of strength I think of Dad.

'Your father's a strong man,' I've often been told. 'He won't let us down.' He is a strong man, I know – but perhaps I choose to view his strength in a different light from many of his admirers who seem to find only its advantages in Protestant rhetoric. When my father dies, someone will no doubt repeat his words and give them a tone of strength appealing to the heart of staunch Ulster loyalism. I will not care to hear those vain repetitions then, any more than I care for them now, but I will always desire to embrace, to hold with all the love I possess for him as my father; the memory of his strength that performed as much and did well that which he put his hand to. It frightens me sometimes that young men who take a pride in their 'contending for the faith' and in calling themselves 'Paisleyites' don't take a pride in developing the meekness which begets true strength. It is not easy to be read a lecture from someone on the intricasies of your father's beliefs and character and informed in the same breath that they 'know' your father. It seems their preconceived ideas make sure they will never 'know' because it is easier to follow blindly than to think! The responsibilities of leadership are vast. My father seeks to make his people think, not just follow. Always there will be some who are content just to follow, but for those who take his leadership and think, the wealth of their future will not lie in rhetoric but in the truths he has sought to uphold.

Fame, as the world knows it, has come for Dad through no accidental circumstance. It has been the by-product of careful observation, skilful consideration and hours of study, the final results of which will be a betterment of life for many generations of people. Fame has come quicker for others who have associated themselves with his leadership – for some it came too quickly and the fading trace of light as they plummeted marked their transient strength. It takes tremendous stamina to cope with all that is entailed in Ulster's politics. I think it takes too much.

Don't get the wrong impression though. Dad has never gone after fame and recognition. No-one seems to grasp the fact that

Dad never sat down when a young man and decided to found his own party and denomination. Circumstance and events brought from him an active response, which in turn motivated others to support and act with him. Things happened. That is what I thoroughly enjoy about Dad. He thinks and acts. He doesn't think and remain static like so many, nor does he think and permit thinking to render him useless.

He really isn't into status or position holding and his career evidences his contempt of ambition over principle. Many within even our own party are into political position-holding, I know. The DUP is no different from any other party in that respect. It has the same mixture of characters and the same diversities of opinion. That is good and necessary for any organisation. What I most detest in Ulster politics is the man who claims to be in politics for 'the Cause', but whose walk blatantly contradicts this. Why he doesn't just admit he enjoys politics and has ambition in that area baffles me. Where is the sin in wanting to make politics your career any more than engineering or architecture or anything else? I must repeat, though, that Dad is about the farthest thing you could get from a career politician.

Dad's greatest asset, and not just politically, he says, is Mum. In this disgruntled, weary, ambitious old world, it is a pleasure to come home to someone whose loyalty is not such that it views everything with a rosy tint nor which overlooks faults and realities, but whose love and discernment make her not just an equal partner but also a *confidante*. Solace, joy and practical help are fruits of such a relationship, and any politician who hasn't this support must surely envy Dad. Many a man's wife has led to his downfall, but conversely, many a man's wife has made him the man he is.

The hallmark of Dad's life is that he has time for people. His time is spent on others. People are the only eternal objects we touch. Nothing else goes into eternity with us. The realisation of this fact ought to prompt us to love dearly our family members, friends and neighbours, and to make time for one another. What a different society would exist if we consciously made this the theme of daily living! It is easy to respond when you disagree or oppose. If half the eagerness we had was used to thank and to encourage, the spreading of goodwill would, I reckon, heal half the broken-hearted and damaged people around us in just one fell swoop. Taking time to listen, to have a 'wee yarn' as they say here, is more vital today than ever. At any time Christ may arrive, or may choose to bring us to him by death – and what does a Christian do? How does he occupy his time? I'm afraid we all just rush around from task to task – hardly taking the time to get there, and certainly not prepared to stop and talk to people on the way. We all like to be loved, but it is a two-way thing; we lack in it because we are simply not prepared to give time to it. There are plenty of people who will sail along with you on the crest of your wave, but surprisingly few stay around if a storm breaks and you need help riding it out. Not many like getting dirty digging ditches, yet they are all happy to use the water supply.

Honest communication has made our home what it is. We are an ordinary family and we have divers ways of reacting, behaving and coping. We hold strong views and opinions, all of which are by no means the same. Because Dad, as head of our home, has ordered his steps correctly, what we have in love for one another surpasses whatever else comes our way.

One of the hardest aspects I find of the youth work I do is keeping from taking on the habits and attitudes of those I am constantly with: language is so easy to pick up, as is gesture and response. You simply cannot work among any group of people without succumbing to their influence to some extent. To glean the good and reject the contaminating is easier said than done, yet that is exactly what I see in Dad's life. He mixes with all 'kinds, colours and creeds' so to speak. He learns from them, discerns, and then uses what he has learnt, not to the detriment but to the strengthening of his character.

In this book, I have tried not to paint a rosy picture of any aspect of our life as a family. That would be a pointless endeavour; anyway, to sustain chapters full of some invented picture would be beyond my writing skills. The pattern of my father's life before us has been that of a good man whose steps are ordered by his Lord. He has taught us to keep close to

Christ and not put our confidence in men. He knows we often need a strong hand, but when he has extended his hand to do that parental duty, it is a hand that readily draws us back to him in an embrace. I know he feels for our defeats and sorrows, and I know he delights in seeing our successes and desires fulfilled. I have only one regret as his child, and that is that I do not trace a closer pattern to all he and Mum have done for me and mean to me. As parents they have guided each of us five children on to the surest, unfailing foundation a person can have. That place is the cleft of the rock carved out by a Redeemer's supreme sacrifice for our sins. Our places are unique to us and our names engraved on the palm of his hand. With ever increasing demands upon us as a family, the hiding place to which we can retreat is quite simply our sole means of survival, restitution and hope.

> Rock of ages cleft for me,
> Let me hide myself in thee;
> Let the water and the blood,
> From thy riven side which flowed,
> Be of sin the double cure,
> Cleanse me from its guilt and power.
>
> Nothing in my hand I bring,
> Simply to thy cross I cling;
> Naked, come to thee for dress,
> Helpless, look to thee for grace;
> Foul, I to the fountain fly,
> Wash me, Saviour, or I die.
>
> Not the labour of my hands
> Can fulfil thy laws demands;
> Could my zeal no respite know,
> Could my tears forever flow,
> All for sin could not atone;
> Thou must save and thou alone.
>
> While I draw this fleeting breath,

When my eyelids close in death;
When I soar to worlds unknown,
See thee on thy judgement throne,
Rock of ages, cleft for me,
Let me hide myself in thee.

★ *Then above the world and sin,*
Through the veil, drawn right within,
I shall see Him face to face,
Sing the story saved by grace,
Rock of ages, cleft for me,
Let me ever be with thee.

★ This verse was written by Dad.

Whatever you may think of my father's political aims or religious beliefs, I trust that you will not permit those views to rob you of the view of him in the softer tones of a husband, father and friend.

★

Cherith, who is a supporter of Greenpeace, one day purchased for herself and me some brightly coloured Greenpeace car stickers. The same day she gave Dad a lift, and of course he couldn't miss the thing staring him in the face.

'My goodness,' he exclaimed 'I hope you're not getting involved in that. I don't want any political activists in my family!'

Poor Dad has never been allowed to forget that statement. Every time there is a protest or controversy raging, we tell him.

'My goodness, we don't want any political activists in our family!'